PRAISE FOR *BARE KNUCKLE PEOPLE MANAGEMENT*

"Coaching a professional basketball team is not different from managing a team of corporate employees. On a basketball team you have stars, utility players, and bench warmers, all of whom thrive when their coach tailors his approach to their unique talents, weaknesses, and contributions to the team. *Bare Knuckle People Management* speaks directly to managers who have been frustrated by the notion that all employees need to be treated equally and with kid gloves."

—Mike D'Antoni, Head Coach of the New York Knicks

"The school of hard knocks approach to the challenges of managing the team you are given. *Bare Knuckle People Management* helps you to develop strategies to optimize the performance of the team by assessing the strengths and weakness of each member of the group. The good news is that all of this advice is actionable now for managers—not just at annual reviews or after expensive assessment surveys!"

—Kevin A. Schulman, MD, Professor of Medicine,
and Gregory Mario and Jeremy Mario Professor of
Business Administration, Duke University

"*Bare Knuckle People Management* is a knock-out! Authors Sean O'Neil and John Kulisek deliver a writing style that entertains while providing useful insights on how to get the most from your team (of inevitably unique personalities). After reading this book, you will be better prepared to confront the 'people challenges' that often prevent managers from maximizing their effectiveness. *Bare Knuckle* is a must-read for anyone who manages people in your organization."

—Philip Pecora, President & CEO Genesee Regional Bank

"*Bare Knuckle People Management* is a clever, straight-forward, practical guide to understanding and managing each of your people to get the most out of them. A refreshing break from 'leadership books' that insist the key to management success is a one-size-fits-all formula. Finally, a book that speaks directly to the manager for the real world."

—Christopher Heck, Senior Vice President of the
National Basketball Association

"The authors of *Bare Knuckle People Management* know successful people management is easier than a lot of managers make it. Kulisek and O'Neil's no-nonsense insights are not only amusing but on the mark. If you are a manager looking to improve the performance of your team, someone who just became a manager or think you would like to become a manager, you will be glad you read this book."

—Paul Mott, Head of Club Services, Major League Soccer

"*Bare Knuckle People Management* is the top solution for the most common people-management issues. It provides the specific distinctions needed to turn your management into leadership. Read this book and watch your teams succeed!"

—Justin Sachs, bestselling author of
The Power of Persistence and *Your Mailbox Is Full*

"Forget Leadership Training! This is how to hit the ground running as a manager. Every sentence provides realistic, practical, and applicable advice for today."

—Ivan Dunmire, EVP, Director of Human Resources, MPG

"Creating success with the team you have is probably the most problematical challenge for every manager. Say goodbye to cheesy team-building exercises and say hello to methods that truly work.

Bare Knuckle People Management is an indispensable resource to taking your entire team to the next level."

—Barry Moltz, author of *Getting Small Business Unstuck*,
Speaker and Consultant

"Very entertaining and informative! *Bare Knuckle People Management* takes a hard fist to the soft science of management, giving the reader practical advice on how to get the most out of a team of differing personalities and skill sets. The characterization of the possible employees that could make up your team at work is dead-on, and anyone who has a bit of sports acumen or pop-cultural awareness will be able to identify with them with ease thanks to the examples in the book. *Bare Knuckle People Management* should be the foundation for any college's Management 101 class."

—Mike Gutch, CFO NewsCore

BARE KNUCKLE
PEOPLE MANAGEMENT

Creating Success with the Team
You Have—Winners, Losers,
Misfits, and All

Sean O'Neil and John Kulisek

BenBella Books
Dallas, Texas

BenBella Books, Inc.
10300 N. Central Expressway, Suite 400
Dallas, TX 75231
www.benbellabooks.com
Send feedback to feedback@benbellabooks.com

Printed in the United States of America
10 9 8 7 6 5 4 3 2 1

Library of Congress Cataloging-in-Publication Data is available for this title.
978-1-935618-485

Cover design by Faceout
Text design and composition by Yara Abuata
Printed by Berryville Graphics

Distributed by Perseus Distribution
(www.perseusdistribution.com)

To place orders through Perseus Distribution:
Tel: 800-343-4499
Fax: 800-351-5073
E-mail: orderentry@perseusbooks.com

Significant discounts for bulk sales are available. Please contact Glenn Yeffeth at glenn@benbellabooks.com or (214) 750-3628

To my family: Pam, Ariana and Zachary. It is all for you.
—JOHN

To my wife, Erin, and my children, Matt, Ryan, Julia, and Olivia.
Still trying to figure out what I did to deserve all of you.
—SEAN

Acknowledgments

The Authors would like to thank the following people for their help on this project, without whom we this book might never have been published:

To our smart, savvy, and cleverly funny agent, Susan Ginsburg, and her team at Writers House. You believed in us when we feared no one else would, and gave us a chance at the big leagues.

To our undyingly patient and brilliant publishing team at BenBella Books, specifically Glenn Yeffeth, Debbie Harmsen, and Adrienne Lang. You met to coddle us when we were down. You kept us in check when we acted like author divas. And, most of all, you managed us through this strange and arduous process of publishing a book. You made this book infinitely better.

To our steady, self-assured publicity compass, Angela Hayes and her team at Goldberg McDuffie. You were willing to dream big like we do.

To all of our friends and family who gave us support and feedback from the moment this project took shape. Specific thanks to Greg Anastas, Matt O'Neil, Jeff Kulisek, Steve Wendell, and Tamiko Benjamin, the ones who read the early, ugly drafts and helped us deliver a product that we could proudly take to market; and to Bruce Dunbar, without whom we would never have gotten within a whisker of meeting Susan Ginsburg.

Personal Acknowledgments

From J.K.

To Bruce, Alan, Linda, Norman, and Evelyn Adler. Without you I have no idea where I would be. Thank you for all of the opportunities and guidance you have given me over the past two decades.

To Steve and Rayna, Alan and Cory, Joey and Prudence, Kendra and Penny, and Curt and Cindy. We have all gotten older and better together. Good times in the past and many more to come as we watch our families grow and continue to amaze us. You were all there when it was good AND when it was bad. Thanks for your loyalty and support.

To Jordan Adler and Leo Efstathiou for your motivation. My contribution to this endeavor is a direct result of trying to keep pace with both of you. Your future is bright boys... wear shades!

To Carl Mancini, Devon Lane, Previn Smith, Paul Franke, and Vince Livoti. There through thick and thin and always "got" me when others didn't. I am here for whatever, whenever.

To Jeff, Tia, Mom, My Grandmother Clara Kulisek, Dad, Jane, Vinnie, Lena, and all my aunts, uncles, and cousins. Being related to me is never an easy thing but being related to some of you isn't all it's cracked up to be either. So cut me some slack.

Finally, to Sean O'Neil, for not only including me in your project but allowing me to share the full credit with you on the cover. This is just your first step in what is sure to be an extraordinary writing career. One thing I am sure of... no matter how well we do as a team, coach Herb Roth would STILL have something negative to say.

From S.O.

I find myself indebted to entirely too many people, but feel compelled to mention a few by name:

To those in my professional past and present who have taught me lessons I call on every day. Specific thanks to Jade McGleughlin, the best damn manager I ever had, who helped me locate the confidence to confront, whom I curse for giving me the irreversible power of insight, and who I'm quite sure never thought she'd be acknowledged in a business book; to David Furman and Andy Levy, who were unable to instill their love of the law in me, but who nevertheless unwittingly became my first management training clients; and to Chris Briller, for offering the opportunity of a lifetime, and for never letting me forget that it's not as easy as it looks.

To my dear friends, who continue to give me more than I could ever give them. Special mention to Gerry DiMarco, my unofficial (and unpaid) therapist, business consultant, and confidante; and the Philly Six, who are my nine Pelham brothers.

To Dad, Scott, Mike, Matt, and Shannon, my family members that keep me forever focused and driven. Being surrounded by such wonderful and successful people my whole life, you are constant reminders of my family obligation to step up.

To Mom, for never losing the faith that I could take the family business to a different place. You turned my back surgery rehab into a career and life overhaul. Thanks for rescuing me.

Finally, to John Kulisek, for finding me on Facebook and reminding me where my roots originated. If not for you, this book would still be locked somewhere on my hard drive. Thanks for breathing new life into it and for catering to my limitless ego.

BARE KNUCKLE
PEOPLE MANAGEMENT

Table of Contents

Introduction

Why You? Why Now?

If you're like most managers, you have spent at least a little time wondering why the hell you ever left the wonderful world of non-management. You were among your company's best employees right up until the day you were promoted. You blew past performance hurdles, exceeded quotas, impressed execs with your diligence and work ethic, and were slated for greatness almost from the minute your employment began. Then suddenly, precisely because of your frontline success, you were plucked to manage a group of poor slobs struggling to survive in the very job in which you thrived. Just as quickly, you ceased being the company darling. You might have even flirted with the chopping block.

Managers often struggle with how to transfer their frontline skills into middle management success. What qualified as drive and peskiness in your last job is viewed as ruthlessness and inflexibility in your management role. You were once the poster child for success, so you can't understand why the hell your assigned disciples don't just snap to and do what you tell them to do. You're offering them the Holy Grail to success, imparting the wisdom of someone they ought to emulate, and they're not taking it!

So maybe the brass recognized these transitional challenges, and sent you to leadership training. Oh, that went well. After learning the benefits of group hugs and all the words to "Kumbayah," you returned to the office with doubts about everything—your ability to manage people, your employer's sensibility, even your faith in humanity. No, you definitely don't want to reread *How Full Is Your Bucket*. That approach is just not for you. Guess what … it's probably not for your team, either.

Of course people generally *like* to be spoken to nicely.

Of course they generally *prefer* praise to criticism.

Of course they generally *like* it better when their boss is more like John Wooden than Bobby Knight.

The question you're validly left asking is whether doing what your employees *like* actually yields results. Who cares if your employees hate you? Don't employees need discipline and structure? Don't they need to be held accountable? You've got your own handful of compelling anecdotes that suggest cracking the whip yields a better return on your time than doling out warm fuzzies. Your gut and experience are telling you one thing, while today's pontificating gurus are telling you quite another. Do you really need advice from the ivory tower? Common sense, after all, is common sense.

> Before you landed the promotion, your success rose and fell with you and only you. Now you need to depend on these poor excuses for employees to make you look good. Yikes!

Before you landed the promotion, your success rose and fell with you and only you. Now you need to depend on these poor excuses for employees to make you look good. Yikes!

But you're a go-getter, not a whiner, so when your first approach failed, you decided to try some new things. In fact, you've tried everything. You've tried whipping them. You've tried hugging them. You've tried drinking with them. You've tried micromanaging them. But the results are too slow in coming. They don't seem to care as much as you do, and you're starting to wonder if you should just go back to doing the frontline thing—the very thing that you were so good at before you entered the management ranks.

Wait…deep breath…

What if we told you that you already know how to manage your team? That almost all of your most valued skills—accurately surveying and responding to the workplace dynamics that surround you, and consistently delivering precisely what everyone around you needs from you—are really, actually fully transferable to management? What if we told you that you could continue to be you (not some warm fuzzy dork that your leadership trainers want you to be) and be as great a manager as you were an entry-level employee?

Do It Your Way

The question that most managers want to know the answer to is *"Must I do it 'their' way?"* The answer—and the central tenet of this book—is a resounding "NO!"

You do it any way you want. You don't need to pretend to be someone you're not. You just need your team to perform well so you look good. But keep this in mind: the best thing you can do for yourself (and your team) is to get the best performance out of as many of your people as you possibly can. And because people by their very nature are so complex, what works for one employee will not likely work for another. No matter what your tendencies and inclinations, understanding the drivers of each person and tailoring your approach accordingly is most likely to maximize individual and team performance (and therefore your income and career success).

This in and of itself might sound "fluffy" to you. You might be saying, "Why do I have to adjust to them? I'm the boss, right? They should be adjusting to me!" The truth is that now that you're managing others, you're no longer in complete control over your own performance results. That is, for the first time in your illustrious career, you are relying on others—your team—to deliver results for you, and this gives them a fair amount of leverage over you. If they're not buying what you're selling, they can hurt you. Demanding they conform to your style is likely to be met by underperformance and, in the worst case, mass exodus.

Look, you don't deal with each of your siblings the same way. You don't treat each of your children the same way. Why would you apply a blanket approach to managing people who have absolutely nothing in common other than who signs their paychecks?

Look, you don't deal with each of your siblings the same way. You don't treat each of your children the same way. Why would you apply a blanket approach to managing people who have absolutely nothing in common other than who signs their paychecks?

We begin this book with our People Principles, a useful list of our management guidelines that will help you understand where we're coming from.

In part 2, "Your Workplace Winners, Losers, Misfits, and All," we lay out a wide array of employee character profiles, several of which will seem hauntingly familiar to you ("Hey wait! How the hell do they know Sam?!"). We:

- Name them (our favorite part)
- Describe them so you know them when you see them
- Identify workplace environments in which these characters tend to thrive and falter
- Propose management strategies that will help you get more productivity from them

The point is not to neatly fit everyone into a character profile. Some members of your team will fit squarely into one profile, some will be a combination of a few, and still others are so, um...how can we politely say this?...distinctive (you know who we mean) that they cannot be safely categorized with anyone else, and probably warrant a full battery of psychiatric exams. We want to heighten your awareness of the individual needs of your people and improve your ability and willingness to customize your management approach to them accordingly.

In part 3, our "Teams" section, we help you fully comprehend the way in which your particular characters blend together and how you can use this insight to make the most of your group's dynamic. You will gain a better understanding of which levers to pull and which to leave untouched, and how to best use your time with this particular mix of employees.

And finally, for those who are expecting to become managers for the first time, or those who are expecting a lateral move to manage another team and are expecting a call from a company executive imminently, we offer up a strategy for your first thirty days on the job. We give you some out-of-the-box considerations that should let you hit the ground running and effortlessly accelerate to full speed.

> *We want to help YOU get better performance from each person on your team so YOUR results improve and YOU quickly return to star status in the minds of your company executives.*

You'll note that some of our recommendations have the unintended consequences of making some of your employees "feel good," but make no mistake about our intended consequences of writing this book: We want to help YOU get better performance from each person on your team so YOUR results improve and YOU quickly return to star status in the minds of your company executives.

This book is intended to liberate. That's right—from here on out you have permission to act solely in your self-interest. So go ahead, throw out the leadership books written by Dr. Feelgood.

You are here, and the time is now. Turn the page.

PART I

THE PEOPLE PRINCIPLES

An Overview

Our People Principles shape the way we think about—and encourage you to think about—managing your people.

We refer to them as "principles" because we think of them not as hard and fast rules to be applied absolutely in all situations, but as useful guidelines and considerations. They are our framework for helping you get more of what you want from your employees. Some of our People Principles might threaten your long-held beliefs about management and corporate authority. That's completely okay. Remember, we give you license to disagree with us.

As with everything we set forth in this book, treat our People Principles like you would, say, a Vegas brunch buffet:

1. Take a look at everything before you put anything on your plate.
2. Take a lot of what you know you want and sample stuff you want to try.

3. Come back as often as you like to have more of whatever you enjoyed the first time, or try something new. No matter what, be sure you eat plenty and leave satisfied!

Managers who understand what they're doing and why—even if it's wildly different from how and why we would manage—are better equipped to clearly communicate their philosophy, make strategic and tactical policy decisions, and realize consistent performance from their teams.

So take a moment to peruse our People Principles. Think about them. Play with them. Take what fits you and your team, sample whatever looks interesting, and discard the rest. Frankly, feel comfortable discarding them altogether, and recognize up front that the way you think about management is just plainly different from the way we do.

At the very least, if you have never before articulated your own "management principles"—your underlying philosophy of managing your team—we hope the following People Principles give you the inspiration to do so. Managing without an underlying philosophy leads you to make impulsive, inconsistent, and regrettable decisions. Managing without this kind of a rudder is like piling your plate high with the prime carving station meats at the Vegas buffet because it's the first thing you see and you're starving, and then realizing on your way back to your seat that they have the choicest cuts of sushi you've ever seen. Doh!

Managing without an underlying philosophy leads you to make impulsive, inconsistent, and regrettable decisions. Managing without this kind of a rudder is like piling your plate high with the prime carving station meats at the Vegas buffet because it's the first thing you see and you're starving, and then realizing on your way back to your seat that they have the choicest cuts of sushi you've ever seen. Doh!

People Principle #1

Team-Wide Rules Suck

Scrutinize team-wide rules very carefully and avoid instituting them wherever possible. Rules are everywhere, and for good reason—they tend to drive (or discourage) behavior for a good chunk of the population. Take mandatory study hall in high school, for example. It's safe to assume that most high school students spend most of their mandatory study hall time studying or doing homework. So mandatory study hall drives most students to participate in the desirable behavior of studying.

But mandatory study hall does not drive desired behavior in *all* high schoolers. What about the kids who skip study hall? Or those who use the time to secretly text friends? Or those who do complete their homework in study hall but do so at the expense of doing it at home, where they do their best work? Or those who would make better use of that time by taking more challenging classes and stretching their intellectual limits?

Standing Monday morning team meetings are the same as mandatory study halls. Sure, everyone gets to work on time because of the meeting, they understand your initiatives for that week, and they come together as a team. And plenty of your team members probably find real value in it. But what about your star employee (we call him Franchise), who has his most productive stretches during that time of day? Or the one who disrupts the meeting because she finds them a waste of her time? Or the one who is too intimidated to ask you questions in the larger group but might in a smaller group of equally uncertain peers?

NOTE

We're *not* saying not to hold regular team meetings and require attendance. We are saying, understand the unintended consequences of doing so, and be aware of the value of that meeting for each person. Weigh those factors against your perceived value of the meeting for all, and *then* decide whether you're going to insist on attendance.

Let's say you managed a team of sales reps, and you instituted a rule that required all reps to bring proposals to you for your approval before sending them on to prospects. At first glance, this team-wide rule might make sense. You want to ensure that proposals are professional and present the company in the best possible light, that pricing contemplates sufficient profit margin and likelihood of securing the business, and that your people are delivering enough proposals to generate sales to justify their presence on your team. But look at the potential costs of instituting this rule:

1. Delays in getting the proposals out because they're backed up on your desk might cost you sales.

2. Your best reps might become frustrated by this time-wasting "micromanagement" requirement of yours and seek to leave their jobs.

3. Some reps who know that you will be reviewing the proposals will grow reliant on you for editing and therefore deliver to you increasingly unpolished work that costs you more time on each one.

It would be a far more efficient strategy for you to require certain reps—your newest, laziest, or poorest proposal writers—to run their proposals by you, while giving those who know what they're doing the ball and letting them run with it. As your newbies, lazies, and poor proposal writers demonstrate competence, you can loosen the reins on them as well.

Rules almost never shape behavior for an entire population... as a manager of a small team of ten to fifteen employees—not "masses"—you can actually be more efficient by limiting hard-and-fast rules to a short list.

Rules almost never shape behavior for an entire population. High schools, like governments and HR departments, benefit from wide-reaching rules because they do shape behavior for the masses—the rules make organizations and people operate efficiently! But as a manager of a small team of ten to fifteen employees—not "masses"—you can actually be more efficient by limiting hard-and-fast rules to a short list. You can afford to take the time and tailor rules to fit each person under your charge.

Because you know the strengths, weaknesses, and drivers of each team member (or you will after reading this book), you are more likely to drive (or discourage) the behaviors you want (or don't want) by simply customizing your policies for each.

REMEMBER

By avoiding team rules, you cut down on time-wasting enforcement and get more from each employee.

People Principle #2

Own Your Own Shit

Some people really suck. You know the ones. You see them walking down the hall, and your first impulse is to dive into the nearest cubicle before they see you so you don't have to actually talk to them. This is a problem—especially when they report to you! Every manager we've ever spoken with has endless stories about the "types" of employees they are forced to deal with on a daily basis but would rather not. This list includes:

- The uncertain sort who insists on having a manager weigh in on every decision (see Needy Ned's profile in the Benchwarmers section of part 2).

- The arrogant newbie who insists on doing it his way, and only his way, even though he has no idea what he's doing (see The Future in the Starting Five section of part 2).

- The overly sensitive employee who bursts into tears every time he hears constructive feedback (see Steady Eddie in the Utility Players section of part 2).

Well, we've got news for you: every employee we've ever spoken with has endless stories about their nightmare boss (and when they see their boss walking down the hall, the cubicle dive appeals to them, too). Ones they frequently mention:

> *It takes two to tango... before you go about "correcting" your employees' faults and avoiding certain people altogether, take a minute to objectively reflect on anything you're doing (or not doing) or saying (or not saying) that is making their behavior worse.*

- The micromanager who insists that her people account for every minute of every day (they call you "The Fuzz").
- The compulsive nice guy who places employee approval over sound business decisions (they call you "Mr. Softy").
- The screamer who regularly and unpredictably unloads on unsuspecting reps (they call you "An Asshole").

The takeaway here? It takes two to tango. Yes, there are loser employees out there, and they would be losers no matter who was managing them. But before you go about "correcting" your employees' faults and avoiding certain people altogether, take a minute to objectively reflect on anything you're doing (or not doing) or saying (or not saying) that is making their behavior worse. The better you understand your own contributions to the dynamic gone bad, the better equipped you'll be to effectively address an individual's negative actions.

Being armed with insight into your own behavior might pave the way for you to give very useful feedback to the employee about the effect his behavior has on you.

Here's an example:

YOU: John, every time I see you walking toward me I try to duck into a cubicle so you don't see me first.

EMPLOYEE: I know, Boss, I've seen you do it. That pisses me off and hurts my feelings. Why do you do that?

YOU: There's no good reason. But I think it's because you tell those endless stories about your cats. I've got a lot of shit on my plate, and I'm usually feeling pressed for time. I feel like I've tried to indicate as much to you, but my hints haven't seemed to register.

EMPLOYEE: Hmm. I'm a little embarrassed. I thought you liked my stories about Mitsy and Ditsy. You always nod and smile and ask questions.

YOU: I never want to be rude, especially when you seem to enjoy telling them so much. I realize I may have been encouraging, not discouraging, the behavior, and that has sent me diving for the cubicles … which is why I'm telling you now. We're in a nasty little pattern.

EMPLOYEE: Well, I will certainly stop sharing cat stories and will try to be more aware when you're in a hurry. I'd love it if you would just tell me when you don't have the time.

When managers fail to recognize their own contributions to bad boss-employee dynamics, they often head down the unsightly and slippery slope called "performance management" actions, which too often result in an employee quitting or getting fired. That might be okay—especially if the person really drives you crazy—but it probably costs you considerably to recruit and get a replacement up to speed for that departed worker. You will see radically improved results if you take stock of your own behavior and factor it in before confronting the target employees head on. And even if nothing changes, owning your own shit has cost you very little and gives you the possibility of a healthy return.

REMEMBER

The more you are able to acknowledge and recognize your own contributions to bad boss–employee interactions, the better equipped you'll be to objectively address your employees' problematic behaviors.

People Principle #3

Look for Leverage Everywhere...
and Exploit It Like Crazy

Management leverage (*noun*):
an advantageous condition in which a manager is positioned to exert a relatively small amount of time and energy that will yield him a relatively high return

Discouraging or reinforcing an employee's behavior is so much easier than most managers make it look. Once you determine what each person wants and doesn't want, you can implement a highly customized system of carrots and sticks that effectively shape each individual's behavior. At the end of the day, you're their boss, and ultimately you have significant influence over their career paths, image among higher-ups, access to certain company perks, etc.

As part of your one-on-one meetings with your team members, take some time to find out what makes each of them tick. Find out about their personal lives, career aspirations, internal and external pressures, and trigger points. These will be very useful to you, as you need them to move in a particular direction.

Think like the parents of a five-year-old child as everyone's finishing off pumpkin pie on Thanksgiving night. They ask their kid what he wants for Christmas...and the kid sings like a canary. Fast forward two weeks later at the mall when the kid starts throwing a fit because Santa is on a long break and the parents have to race home to get ready for the office holiday party. "Now little Johnny, Santa might not be here now, but you know he's watching. And if he doesn't see you pull it together real soon, he'll never bring you the new soldier fort you were hoping to get." It works like a charm.

Once you determine what each person wants and doesn't want, you can implement a highly customized system of carrots and sticks that effectively shape each individual's behavior.

Your employees are no different. Ellen, who has made it very clear in her one-on-ones with you that she wants you to submit her name as a management candidate when a position opens up, has given you a huge hunk of leverage. So when she fails to take an active mentorship role with the newbies you asked her to look after, you can dangle the management position in front of her to get her re-engaged: "Ellen, I'm noticing that our newbies could benefit from someone taking them under her wing. This might be just the display of leadership that I can reference when my boss comes to me looking for management candidates."

One more very important note about leverage: just because you maintain a direct management position over someone does not mean that leverage lies in your favor—you might need to look high and low for leverage of your own.

Think of your Franchise employee. He carries your team and makes you look good because of his high level of production. He's regarded highly by everyone inside and outside the company. Headhunters have his number on speed dial. In order to establish a leverage point with Franchise, you need to create real value for him so that without you, his work experience would be quantifiably less good. You might process his work orders, or take on his interdepartmental battles, or carve out an attractive career path possibility for him, or lobby aggressively for a better comp plan for him. Yes, he works for you, but every Franchise worth his weight in salt knows that you really work for him, and that he can successfully market himself to the highest-bidding manager inside or outside your company. In order for you to continue to reap the benefits of Franchise's productivity, you need to periodically exert energy in ways that reminds Franchise of the value you bring versus that of other potential managers.

Leverage is infinitely less complicated for your less dependable characters, like Slacker. The leverage calculation in these relationships is plain—you are the boss and you hold their jobs in your hands. But, just as you did with Franchise, you get to know what drives them, and you can use that knowledge to get more out of them. Here's an example of how you can take this leverage out for a spin with Slacker:

You: Hi, Slacker, good to see you. Not sure if you're aware, but you managed to get into work on time and stay here for the entire work day this whole week.

Slacker: Dude ... are you serious?

You: Yes. I can't remember the last time that happened. I'd like to see more of this, so I thought I would dangle a little carrot in front of you.

Slacker: A beer might be more enticing, Boss.

You: Now, now, Slacker. I was thinking something more like a golf outing.

Slacker: Dude ... I freaking love golf.

You: Yes, I know. You spent more afternoon time on the golf course than Phil Mickelson last spring. But you've been picking it up a notch, and I want to recognize that effort—and see it continue. Slacker, if you give me uninterrupted attendance—steady work all day, every day—over the next three weeks, I'll have you represent our office in the industry golf outing next month. Deal?

Slacker: Dude…that's totally a deal.

Conceptually, the very idea of exercising management leverage makes some managers squirm. Some say it's manipulative and can lead to abuse of power. Okay, we accept that. But being cognizant of where the leverage lies with each of your employees and how to mobilize it to get more of what you want from them can be among your most valued management tools.

And we're not suggesting for a moment that you pretend to be Snow White while maliciously and discreetly yanking your employee's strings to get them to perform tricks for your own amusement. (We leave that to elected officials.) We're suggesting that power dynamics in the workplace (and everywhere else, for that matter) exist, and that to ignore them, or pretend they don't will cost you, your company, and your employees. Your heightened awareness of them as they pertain to the individuals you manage will yield you better performance from each.

REMEMBER

Leverage exists in every relationship, and you would do yourself a favor to recognize how it is affecting your work relationships and what you can do to use it to your advantage.

People Principle #4

Talk Often about Large Pink Elephants

No matter how much we try to keep the blinders affixed to the side of our heads, those lurking issues, like two-thousand-pound pink elephants in the room, have a way of creeping into our periphery. The best managers we've encountered not only acknowledge that they exist, but point them out to others. We all know why you don't do it—pink elephants are uncomfortable to talk about and can stir tension and unwieldy emotions that become hard to put away once they're out in the open.

But here's why you must do it: allowing pink elephants to stay in the room, without acknowledgment, permits them to infiltrate interpersonal dynamics, add to existing intra-office tensions, and forge silent but deadly wedges among team players that sap performance and productivity. Pink elephants are giant, silent productivity eaters, and you can't afford not to point them out.

In case you're wondering what in the world we are talking about, we'll roll out an example. Not infrequently, a manager gets promoted to manage the team with which she had been previously working side by side. Not infrequently, one or more people on that team would have liked to have received the same promotion but were passed over. Not infrequently, those passed over kibitz about the one who was promoted and do subtle things to sabotage her new reign.

We're suggesting the new manager face the issue head on. A Pink Elephant Talk among her and her new subordinates might go something like this:

PROMOTED ONE: Hey, thanks for coming in. I need to speak with you about something. Look, I'm sensing a fair amount of tension from you guys since I took over for Paul. I want to get everything on the table now so we can deal with it and move on.

PASSED OVER #1: Tension? What tension? No, we thought you were the perfect choice. God, who would want to deal with all that extra crap you have to deal with anyway. I'm thrilled they didn't ask me.

PASSED OVER #2: Seriously. Like now you actually have to, like, go to meetings at corporate. And you can never wear open-toe shoes there. Who could possibly want that? Honestly, I don't know what you're talking about.

PROMOTED ONE: Um, right. But I saw a copy of the petition you two drafted to have me removed and you two installed as co-managers. It only had two signatures on it... and they were yours.

PASSED OVER #1 AND #2: (Silence.)

PROMOTED ONE: Look, I get it. I'm not sure how I would have responded if I were in your shoes (open-toed or not). All I know is that if we all do well, then we all look good. And if we all do poorly, then we all look really, really bad. If you're pissed off about my getting promoted, then let's have a discussion about it. We can even see if there's a way I can position you guys for the next promotion that gets posted. But we need to avoid beating each other up behind each other's backs.

Or how about those delicate discussions you need to have when one's personal hygiene is getting in the way of his performance? That might go something like this:

You: I think we need to talk.

Pig Pen: Sure, Boss. Oh, looks like you missed a spot shaving.

You: Right. Well, funny you should say that. I actually wanted to speak with you about your hygiene...and shaving is one of the concerns I have. You often come to work disheveled and your clothes looking as though you spent the night in the car. I've observed your colleagues commenting on it, and I imagine it's getting in the way of your working with them. Know what I mean?

Pig Pen: Gee, Boss. How do you really feel? Nothing like getting hit between the eyes.

You: I'm sure. You can imagine this is not easy for me either. I wanted to raise it though because this is a departure from what we're used to seeing from you. No one's ever mistaken you for Giorgio Armani around here, but you have historically presented yourself rather professionally. There's been a pretty steep drop-off, and I'm wondering if there's something going on.

PIG PEN: Boss, you might be onto something. My cat, Mitsy, died last month, and ever since I've been up late crying with his twin brother, Ditsy. It's tearing me up inside. I miss that little furball so damn much.

Adopting such a practice may end up shining a light on something that wasn't there to begin with, but by doing so you bring everything into the open for all to see and send the clear message that behind-the-scenes sabotage and hidden agendas will not be tolerated. This has the effect of killing off the unborn pink elephants and angering no one.

REMEMBER

Pink elephants are distracting creatures that wreak havoc on a work environment and grow larger and more distracting the longer they go unaddressed. When you see one—or even if you think you might have seen one—call it out and get your team to focus on the stuff that matters.

People Principle #5

Weigh Words and Tone Carefully

Not everyone is as brash and thick-skinned as you are. In fact, there are some real softies out there—those who look into every spoken and written (and *unspoken* and *unwritten*) word for your validation (or disapproval). They dissect body language, facial expressions, vocal tone, and eye contact. They're watching and listening to everything you do and say, making mental notes and interpreting like crazy. You needn't make yourself as neurotic as they are, but just being more mindful of the impact of the words and tone you use to communicate will help you increase the likelihood of sending them off in a "whole" state, and they'll be able to deliver greater productivity for themselves, for you, and for your company.

In contrast, if you convey your message cavalierly, you risk losing your softies' loyalty and, worse, their performance.

Let's suppose, for example, that you have a very consistent, if unspectacular performer in Steady Eddie, whom you need to assume new responsibilities in order to meet your recently downsized team's needs.

You might say something like this: "Eddie, I need you to do more stuff around here. Time to break out of your comfort zone and really start adding value here. I'm going to have my assistant e-mail you your expanded job description. You can do this!" Many of you would love to get this challenge, but Eddie might be internalizing the wrong messages here:

WHAT YOU MIGHT SAY	WHAT EDDIE MIGHT THINK
"I need you to do more stuff around here."	"I don't contribute enough now."
"Time to break out of your comfort zone."	"I love my comfort zone. Holy shit, I'm terrified when I'm anywhere outside my comfort zone."
"Time to ... really start adding value here."	"That's the second time you said that. Maybe I've never added value here."
"I'm going to have my assistant e-mail you your expanded job description."	"Wait, you're not going to hold my hand through this? I want my mommy."
"You can do this!"	"Yeah, right. Better start looking for a new gig."

So what could you say that would keep Eddie in one piece and still get your point across? How about this: "Eddie, you know everyone thinks the world of you here. You're unbelievably dependable, and everyone, including me, loves you. I also know that you are comfortable in your routine, and you're thriving now. But as you know, we've recently lost a few people, and we need everyone to take on a little bit more work, including you. Why don't we set up some time next week to go through the specific additions to your job description? I'd like to walk you through it, and then put together a detailed phase-in of these responsibilities."

This might be really touchy-feely for you. But this might be what it takes to transition Eddie into his expanded role in a way that doesn't scare him into paralysis or a new job search. Sure, it takes a bit more time and energy from you, and he will need his hand held. But the end result is that you'll lock in a dependable employee for the foreseeable future, and not lose an ounce of productivity from Eddie.

Giving more thought to what you say and how you say it will, even at the margins, help you get it right more often than you would if you paid it no mind at all.

You can certainly make yourself nuts wondering how your softies are going to interpret each and every message you try to convey, and there's no guarantee that you're going to land on the right words and tone. We're just suggesting that giving more thought to what you say and how you say it will, even at the margins, help you get it right more often than you would if you paid it no mind at all. And that just might get you more loyalty, more job satisfaction, and greater productivity.

REMEMBER

Know who needs to be coddled and take a moment to carefully weigh what—and how—you're going to say something to them before you say it.

People Principle #6

Give Individual Feedback Frequently (and Remember That Point about Leverage)

We know what you're thinking: if one more freaking employee complains that they don't get enough quality feedback from you, you're going to quit. Feedback?! You didn't need feedback to be successful, so why should they?

Look, we don't care what the "leadership gurus" say...giving feedback is for *your* benefit, not that of the feedback recipients. People are lab rats whose behavior can be shaped by doling out a pellet or administering a shock based on observed behavior. See behavior you hate? Give feedback so you never see it again. See behavior you love? Give feedback so you see a lot more of it. It's that simple. And that's why the feedback helps you.

Here's how you do it. We call it our "ABC Feedback" method:

A — **ASK** them *if you could directly report some feedback.*

B — *State the employee's observed* **BEHAVIOR** *in objective, unemotional terms.*

C — *Identify the* **CONSEQUENCES** *of the target behavior in a way that, for the specific recipient, is likely to compel them to continue (in the case of a desirable behavior) or stop (in the case of an undesirable behavior) the behavior.*

To put some meat on this, here's an example. Imagine an employee of yours, Joan, who is desperate for a promotion (this is your leverage!), repeatedly shows up late to important team meetings and disrupts them once she arrives. This is problematic for you because Joan's peers look up to her and often follow her lead, so now many team members begin showing up late, or not at all, and disrupt the meeting. Your feedback delivery might go something like this:

YOU: Joan, do you have a minute for some feedback?

JOAN: Sure.

YOU: Great. Joan, for three out of the last four team meetings you arrived after the scheduled start time. Lately, I've noticed some of the newer folks coming late as well. And today, after you got there late, you were joking around with Liz, which disrupted the entire meeting. Joan, you've been after me for months to recommend you for promotion, but it's awfully hard for me to do that when you do things like this. They cause me to question your judgment and leadership ability.

If Joan really does care about getting promoted, and you leverage that information to discourage her undesirable behavior, you're likely to see a change. Now, like employees anywhere, she might give you a bunch of excuses or gooey apologies or complaints about the meetings themselves—any or all of which might merit a longer discussion. But, if she really wants the promotion, you're likely to see her behavior change.

Feedback is so typically negative that employees shudder when they hear the word coming from their bosses' mouths. You can sometimes shock your employees into delivering more of the behavior you want to reinforce through positive feedback.

We'll pick on Joan again in the following example, showing how you can employ positive feedback to encourage more of the behaviors you like.

YOU: Joan, you have a minute for some feedback?

JOAN (still reeling from the last feedback session with you): Um, sure, I guess.

YOU: Great. Yesterday, I was walking by Rosemary's desk, and she was telling Joe that you were instrumental in helping her through a nerve-racking call with an irate customer. She said, "I thought for sure we were going to lose the customer, but Joan saved the day." That sort of selfless act is exactly the type of team behavior I've been trying to instill in all of us since I got here. When I'm looking around the room for new managers, I'm looking for those who display that behavior. Thank you.

If Joan is even remotely committed to getting that promotion, you can bank on seeing much more of that behavior.

REMEMBER

Give your team members feedback for your benefit. It will allow you to see more of the behaviors you want to see and fewer of those you don't.

People Principle #7

Apologize Well... and Then Move On!

Once upon a time, a boss who was copied on a client e-mail (in which his direct report apologized to the client for the employee's oversight) replied with a recommendation for how to respond to future e-mails in similar situations. "Like this..." he wrote. "That way you don't have to apologize to them."

Never being one to miss an opportunity to press his superiors' buttons, the employee quickly shot back, "What the hell is wrong with apologizing?!"

Apologizing gets a bad rap. In our opinion, it's one of the most powerful and efficient interpersonal tools at a manager's disposal. When sensitively delivered, a simple, unqualified apology can magically right a wrong, remind those involved that you are human and subject to lapses in judgment, and, most important, help you get more from those around you. No reason to beat yourself up over your behavior or walk on eggshells after an ugly exchange. State your apology plainly, acknowledge your error, and move on to the business at hand.

Apologies are most effective when they are part of a separate discussion. Example: "Hey, I'm so sorry I lost it yesterday. Lots of stuff weighing on my mind these days, but there's no excuse for that kind of behavior—ever. I'm very sorry. I'll see you later during our one-on-one."

Apologies are most effective when they are part of a separate discussion.

See? Was that so hard? Now the one-on-one can start cleanly and stay focused on business and productivity, where it belongs. In this instance, if you waited until the beginning of the one-on-one, you might have wasted valuable time rehashing a point that should be clearly behind both of you by then.

Some words of caution about apologies:

1. **Don't use apologies as vehicles to restate your position.** Often, managers say something like, "I'm sorry I got a little out of control yesterday, but your lack of explanation about your failure to make quota again was too much to take." This apology threatens to render it, and all future apologies, insincere and useless. Apologies are best when they stand alone.

2. **Don't lean too heavily on apologies.** Like anything good, too many apologies make others tired of them and dilute their magical impact. And then you run the risk of looking less like a manager who cares and more like a manager who's attending an "anger management for dummies" class.

3. **Check for large pink elephants (which often hide behind apologies and bad behavior that lead to them)—see People Principle #4.** Sometimes pink elephants trigger inappropriate responses to certain behavior. Apologies are probably still needed, but then this might be a

time to identify the pink elephant in the room to unearth the underlying tension between you and the recipient.

PART II
YOUR WORKPLACE: WINNERS, LOSERS, MISFITS, AND ALL

An Overview

Okay, you can get your head around this idea of tailoring your style to "sell" your management shtick to each of your people differently. But who are your people? And what on earth are they buying?

Let us guess: you manage a unique collection of knuckleheads. No manager on earth (1) has ever encountered chumps like you've got, or (2) could sell them on the idea of performing better. You know how we know you're thinking that? Because every single manager we've ever met has told us the exact same thing.

In this part of the book, we have an index of sorts—a catalog of workplace character types that we hope you'll find enlightening and amusing. As we indicated in the Introduction, our intention is not that you neatly fit all of your people into one or more of the types described, but that you become skilled at recognizing the different types of people on your team and the infinitely different needs they have of you.

We identify sixteen classic employee character types: Franchise, Legend, Player, Badass, Future, Steady Eddie, Noodler, Doer, Whistler, ADHD Butterfly, Needy Ned, Mr. Inappropriate, Slacker, Burnout, Retread, and Asshole. You've met them all, and you've hired and managed them all (or eventually will). Everyone on your current team fits in here—at least a little bit—somewhere.

Below we give you a brief description of each Workplace Character, and then throughout this part of the book, we flesh out each of these sixteen types and provide useful strategies for getting better performance from each of them.

The Universe of Winners, Losers, Misfits, and All

1 THE FRANCHISE.

May you live to have a Franchise on your team. She is the gold standard. Franchise does it all, and does it exceptionally well. Get out of her way and let her perform. Your only challenge will be keeping things fresh and big enough to keep her.

2 THE LEGEND.

He no longer delivers quite the way he used to, and he's definitely lost a step, but the Legend still has some juice. His deep industry knowledge, and his sterling reputation among peers across company divisions and among customer ranks are reasons enough to keep him happy and on the team.

3 THE PLAYER.

Player makes a stunning first impression and works a room like a pro, flattering everyone he encounters. An impeccable dresser and a verbal acrobat, Player appears a shoo-in for the C-suite. But don't look too hard for depth or substance, because he has little. Player is all sizzle, but the sizzle helps him deliver.

THE BADASS.

She's the proverbial bull in a china shop. Badass knows one direction (straight ahead) and one speed (100 MPH). She'll deliver big results, but she'll also run roughshod over everyone if you let her.

THE FUTURE.

You see pockets of greatness and raw ability with a swagger to match. The Future could become your next Franchise, if only she can check her ego long enough to internalize some best practices.

STEADY EDDIE.

He hits single after single and never wants praise. Steady Eddie keeps a low profile and places the team's needs above his own. Eddie's a little obsessed with process and order, so he's likely to get paralyzed when faced with sudden change. Need predictability? Meet Eddie.

THE NOODLER.

She values precision over just about everything else. Noodler investigates for truth, and can find herself knee-deep in research she gathers to build her case. Her presentations can take hours, with her two hundred-slide PowerPoint shows packed with data on top of analysis.

But don't dismiss Noodler, for every once in a while she'll justify her value by putting forth a thousand-page report that saves the company millions.

THE DOER.

Man, is she busy. She sprints down the hall, gets in at 6 A.M., and sticks around every night long enough to close the place down. Her "To Do" list is always a mile long, and stacks of paper fill her desktop. The problem with Doer, though, is that most of the time she's spending her time working on completely meaningless shit. Her calendar is packed with committee meetings and voluntary cross-divisional conference calls in which she listens with her speaker muted, takes notes, and files them diligently. Get her something material to do, and she'll do it . . . but only if she can find the time.

THE WHISTLER.

Whistler knows the company handbook cold, and she's burned a path to your HR rep's office to report perceived violations. Whistler is hated and feared by most, and the team player in you resents the way she rats out her peers. You have to admit, though, that there are more than a few benefits to having an extra set of eyes and ears out on the floor.

ADHD BUTTERFLY.

He's everywhere—but rarely where you want him to be—and never in any one place for more than three minutes. Butterfly flutters about and talks constantly at the speed of sound about nothing at all. If only you could channel his limitless energy into an activity that rewards such flighty behavior, you just might find reason to get him off the bench.

11 NEEDY NED.

Although he has the tools it takes to make the starting lineup, Needy Ned's anxiety and constant need for approval and assistance keep him on the bench. He has an insatiable appetite for your attention, is afraid of everything, and requires kid glove treatment in order to avoid a display of tears. If you can manage his anxiety and resist the urge to kill, perhaps you could boost his productivity.

12 MR. INAPPROPRIATE.

 Mr. I is the biggest pervert in your shop. He's quick with a dirty joke and a seedy smile. This guy epitomizes old school. Only problem is, his old school classmates have all graduated, and the new crew doesn't appreciate his act.

13 THE SLACKER.

If Slacker spent half the energy working as he spends getting away with not working, he'd be among your very best. Slacker has mastered the discreet Friday afternoon golf outing, and is quicker with a creative new excuse than a finished product. If you didn't love Slacker, he'd be out of a job.

THE BURNOUT.

There was a time when Burnout could deliver, but you can't remember his last good day. Now he wears his fatigue on his sleeve, and you realize the light has been almost completely extinguished. Can you light Burnout's fire again, or is it gone for good?

THE RETREAD.

She's turned twenty jobs in eighteen years and can't identify a notable, verifiable achievement. Somehow (perhaps because she's a professional interviewee) you hired her. This nightmare overpromises and under-delivers, and consumes more negative energy than you can afford to expend.

THE ASSHOLE.

Most offices have one, and they all stink. Asshole doesn't appear to have a redeeming quality. He's rude, abrupt, untrustworthy, and purely self-centered. No one likes him and he doesn't produce, so why the hell does he still work for you?

Categorizing the Crew

We separate the Workplace Characters into four distinct groups:

The Franchise, the Legend, the Player, the Badass, and the Future. These are your go-to guys—the ones you repeatedly depend on to make your number. They're your 20 percent producing 80 percent of the work. Your biggest challenge with your Starters is to keep them happy and interested so they stay on your team and keep on delivering value.

Starting Five

Steady Eddie, the Noodler, the Doer, and the Whistler. This group rarely wows you or your higher-ups. But they each bring unique value that, if strategically leveraged by you, will help you fill specific needs on your team. Think lefty specialist reliever, or the backup quarterback who can run the wildcat near the goal line. Use them well and they will help your team.

Utility Players

ADHD Butterfly, Needy Ned, Mr. Inappropriate, and the Slacker. Most teams are littered with Benchwarmers. Some have potential to see more playing time, but they take a lot of time and energy, and you need to assess in each case whether their replacement cost outweighs the benefits of keeping them around.

Benchwarmers

Trading Block Candidates

The Burnout, the Retread, and the Asshole. It's hard to justify keeping these folks around. Any resources you devote to them seem to go to waste. We are very sensitive to the idea that replacing people is often more costly than keeping around dead weight, but we firmly draw the line at these losers.

STARTING FIVE	UTILITY PLAYERS	BENCHWARMERS	TRADING BLOCK CANDIDATES
The Franchise	Steady Eddie	ADHD Butterfly	The Burnout
The Legend	The Noodler	Needy Ned	The Retread
The Player	The Doer	Mr. Inappropriate	The Asshole
The Badass	The Whistler	The Slacker	
The Future			

Character Profile #1

The Franchise

Starting Five

Utility Players

Benchwarmers

Trading Block Candidates

How Do You Know a Franchise When You See One?

Franchise exudes an inner, earned assuredness that greets you the moment you lay eyes on him. Franchise has always been the favorite child. The teacher's pet. The heartbreaker. And the swagger that develops after a lifetime of ego-building experiences is exactly what makes success come so easily to him. You can't teach or transfer his swagger to others, for it lies deep within his bones and is born of a deep-rooted self-confidence that comes with achievement in every facet and at every stage of life.

You might instantly recognize Franchise because he reminds you of yourself in a previous role, before upper management made the common, but curious, decision to pluck you from the front lines to oversee a team of your peers. You'll notice that Franchise seems to make all the right moves. He knows when to speak and when to keep his mouth shut. He works like a dog, but it appears so effortless. He always delivers—exceptional quality, on time, every time. In fact, Franchise looks so enviably comfortable in his own existence, that he often makes you consider asking for your old job back.

Franchise does not need shout-outs or employee-of-the-month awards. He's bigger and better than that. Consistently awesome results are what he delivers—periodic recognition would almost diminish all he brings to your team and the company.

At his best, Franchise delivers the goods over and over again, exceeding expectations every time. But at his worst, he is a bit too aware of his own market value, and dangles it in front of your face while negotiating for perks that stretch the bounds of your team policies. He might be found peeking around every corner for a bigger stage on which he can showcase his talents.

THE FRANCHISES

WHY YOU LOVE 'EM

- They make you look really, really good.

- They deliver enough value so that whatever your other employees deliver is gravy.

- They provide a benchmark for others.

WHY YOU HATE 'EM

- They might leave you.

- You work for them more than they work for you.

- Good luck delivering them constructive feedback.

Real-life/Screen Examples

- **Michael Jordan**—the gold standard for basketball players... maybe even all professional athletes.
- **Derek Jeter**—try finding a chink in his armor.
- **Denzel Washington**—is he ever bad on the big screen?
- **Oprah Winfrey**—one of the richest women in the world who nevertheless manages to be loved by almost all. Everything she touches turns to platinum.

NBA'S FRANCHISE: MICHAEL JORDAN

Seriously, when is the last time someone has dominated and transformed an industry like Michael Jordan did with the Chicago Bulls? It wasn't just that he was great (shit, you could argue that Chris Webber in his day was great). Jordan defined what all rising ball players aspired to be. His physical attributes, his undeniable talent, his interview poise, and his remarkable grace caused people to stop what they were doing and take him all in. Jordan packed arenas everywhere, and drove playoff television ratings through the roof.

Jordan earned many perks for all of his greatness; he even had a say in how plays were called down the stretch. This was no humble, quiet wallflower. He let you know he was the Bulls' Franchise, and he insisted on star treatment from coaches, teammates... even officials. The regular rules simply did not apply.

Ideal Settings

Franchise is a thriver and one who sees the big picture. So the best settings for Franchise are those in which he is allowed the freedom to creatively apply his many talents and ones in which he isn't mired in details. The key is building a platform large enough for Franchise to achieve his true potential. If Franchise can see that you (and the company) will let him achieve all that he is able to, the chances that he will remain under your employ remain strong.

Franchise will particularly shine in highly visible and important functions. The higher the stakes, the more you can count on Franchise. It's not so much that he needs the spotlight ... it's that he longs to stretch the limits of his capabilities.

Disastrous Settings

If you are unable to let the Franchise spread his wings, then he will find a way out of your pathetic little birdcage and land himself in a spot that will. Tightly contained and scripted environments in which he is not permitted to distinguish himself from his army of peers will drive Franchise batty. The classic Franchise misuse is a factory job in which he is required to plug in the same part two hundred times per day. You won't see him mope (Franchise doesn't mope). You'll see his shine fade and then suddenly, one day soon after, his resignation letter will be on your desk.

Training/Coaching/Monitoring

When it comes to Franchise's development, you might have the impulse to just leave him to his own impressive devices. And who could really argue with that? The only concern here is that Franchise views your hands-off approach as adding no value to him, so when another opportunity with the promise of professional development comes his way, he might just jump ship. Among your biggest challenges is constantly demonstrating the value you bring to Franchise;

professional development is one way to do that. But let's be clear: if Franchise views your attempts at professional development as a waste of his time, you would actually be adding *negative* value! So if you have real value to offer Franchise, find a way to deliver it. If you have nothing of substance, you'll have to demonstrate your value in other ways, such as removing obstacles that tend to stand in the way of his day-to-day productivity.

STRATEGIES FOR MANAGING FRANCHISE

1 Give him room to let him achieve his potential. Hand him a special, high-profile project.

2 Accommodate his needs without caving on all of your policies. (Note: You can set your policies with accommodating Franchise in mind.)

3 Make his life easier by removing obstacles and streamlining productivity efforts. Energy you expend on Franchise will yield a much higher return than the equivalent effort on your Benchwarmers.

4 Find ways to leverage his skills to develop others on the team through team presentations, mentoring, shadowing, etc. As long as Franchise is willing, you might as well use what he's got to bring others along.

5 Think of yourself as Franchise's "partner" as opposed to manager. This will help you catch yourself if you're inclined to manage by enforcement.

(CONTINUED ON FOLLOWING PAGE)

(CONTINUED)

6   Be sure you know what the Franchise wants and needs and then find ways to deliver. Your added value will help cement the relationship and increase the likelihood that Franchise remains a productive member of the team.

7   Promote Franchise's achievements and value to higher-ups and across departments, but be sure to present him as your protégé. You want others to see you as one who develops talent, not one who gets high-quality talent to fall out of the sky onto your team.

If you were a Franchise: find select opportunities to train and mentor Franchise.

8   If you were not a Franchise: avoid training and mentoring opportunities unless you have particular competencies that can be easily transferred to Franchise.

Handling Miscues

You will not encounter many problems with Franchise. The only trouble spots for you will occur when Franchise presses against the limits of your team policies in an effort to leverage all the value he brings you. Don't take this lightly. Yes, we admire the principled managers among you who insist that all your soldiers must fall in line, no matter who they are. But remember, you work for and need Franchise at least as much as he works for and needs you. Ignore his requests for a longer leash at your peril. (Please see our discussion of the Franchise Forgiveness Factor in Team Hickory in part 3 of this book.)

WHAT YOU MIGHT DISCUSS WITH FRANCHISE

YOU: Franchise, didn't see you today at the team meeting. Where were you?

FRANCHISE: Trying to get a deal done, Boss.

YOU: Okay, that's obviously a good use of your time. I know you know I ask everyone on the team to attend that Friday morning meeting. A little heads-up would help me deflect questions from others about why they have to be there if you don't.

FRANCHISE: Look, I'm all for team spirit, Boss, but they need to understand that I've earned the right to forego some of the regular meetings and trainings.

YOU: Of course. I also handle some of your administrative items and fight battles on your behalf behind the scenes. You have earned all of that. All I ask for in return is a little advanced notice so I can head off any questions about your absence.

FRANCHISE: Okay, I can do that.

Character Combinations with Franchise Worth Watching

- **THE FUTURE.** The Future is the best chance you have to create another Franchise. If you have any skills as matchmaker, you need to find ways to make this match and make it work, but it won't be easy. Future might be just arrogant enough to think he can become a Franchise all by himself and dismiss what Franchise has to offer. In addition, Franchise might not deem time with Future a good return on his own valuable time. The key will be your ability to convey to Franchise that Future's brashness has more to do with his insecurities and less to do with irreverence. Good luck with that!

- **THE BADASS.** Badass is so damned competitive that he'll actually dig deep into performance reports to find metrics in which he outperformed Franchise and then parade those around for all to see. Badass's competitiveness usually rolls off Franchise's back, unless, of course, Badass engages in behavior that sabotages Franchise's efforts. These can be tense moments, but they create electrifying fireworks. Badass is accustomed to winning standoffs, but Franchise will not allow anyone to make him look bad. This might be a healthy reality kick to the face for Badass.

- **THE PLAYER.** Franchise immediately sees through Player's thin veneer and is unimpressed by his superficiality. So this interaction would be uninteresting except for Player's incessant and blatant desire to be accepted by Franchise. He bounds after him like a puppy dog and takes Franchise's repeated dismissals hard, which might send Player reeling for a bit. You might need to be there to pick up the pieces.

Keep or Throw Back?

Not all managers are blessed with a Franchise, but those who do have one are well advised to do everything in their power to keep him. Franchise can make a manager's career (think what Phil Jackson would be without Michael Jordan and Kobe Bryant…a mid-tier coach who likes New Age books). If you throw back Franchise, you don't deserve to manage a fish tank full of goldfish.

Character Profile #2

The Legend

How Do You Know a Legend When You See One?

Legend is well dressed, honest, well spoken, professional and, well, old. He knows sports, stocks, politics, jokes, and the most discreet place at headquarters to take a dump. If there is something he doesn't know, you haven't found it yet.

Legend's career is fabled. He holds the patent for the company's defining product line. He made a toast at your biggest client's daughter's wedding. He doles out unused sick days to his colleagues as holiday gifts. He's influential with White House advisors.

Legend is an institution. He was in his prime when your CEO was just a marketing manager. He thrived during the company's boom times and stock splits, and survived the recessions and rounds of layoffs.

Legend commands respect everywhere he goes, and he has earned every damn stitch of it. The problem? Simple. While Legend continues to leverage his seemingly endless Rolodex (yes, he still has a Rolodex) into business, he has stopped moving forward, learning new things, and adapting to a changing workplace, and has no plan to do so now or in the future. Legend is planted firmly in his ways, in ways that make the young bucks roll their eyes and upper management contemplate a variety of severance packages to shed his hefty pay. You, as usual, are caught in the middle.

THE LEGENDS

WHY YOU LOVE 'EM

- They know everyone in the industry and one call from them can change the course of a big deal.

- They monitor themselves while delivering relatively consistent and predictable results.

- They possess knowledge and skill that, if successfully transferred, can radically improve your team's performance.

WHY YOU HATE 'EM

- They can be stingy with their contacts and reputation, but they earned them, after all.

- They bristle at the thought of some punk-kid manager insisting that they submit to training, one-on-ones, and the like.

- Unless there's a clear and sizeable return to them for giving their time and energy to help the team, you're out of luck in getting them to participate.

Real-life/Screen Examples

- **Andy Rooney on** *60 Minutes*—uncomfortably bushy eyebrows and all.

- **Michael Jordan as a Washington Wizard**—still above average but hard to watch nonetheless.

- **Tom Brokaw**—the speech impediment is more noticeable than when in his prime.

- **Clint Eastwood**—still tough, even though he couldn't hurt a flea.

- **Mariano Rivera**—one-pitch wonder, still getting it done.

A LEGEND: ANDY ROONEY

Have you ever wondered how a decrepit old man with comb-over eyebrows and a whiny voice could manage to stay relevant on *60 Minutes*, the world's most watched news magazine? His rants are increasingly more difficult to follow, his references make him seem increasingly dated at best and batty at worst, and we haven't heard a truly funny line leave his lips since the early 1980s. But we watch him week in and week out simply because he's Andy Rooney.

None among us would be surprised at all to be watching one week when, in the middle of a "did you ever wonder" sentence, Andy stops abruptly, keels over right there at his desk on national television, and dies.

(CONTINUED ON FOLLOWING PAGE)

(*CONTINUED*)

What's funny is that many in Generation YouTube, watching him for the first time, would fail to see Andy's genius. Indeed, they might just see a washed-up, nonsensical old man. But those who've been watching Andy for decades still see fleeting bits of the old magic in every monologue. Andy Rooney is a Legend, built two minutes a week on Sunday evenings.

Ideal Settings

Legend thrives in environments in which he is openly appreciated for his vast accomplishments. Legend wants to be one of a small few asked to weigh in on important, game-changing matters, so environments that value input and consensus will appeal to him as well. Look for Legend to be drawn to large industry conferences and trade shows, where he can relive old times with familiar faces, and get star treatment from unfamiliar ones. Keep in mind, however, that you walk a tightrope every time you trot him out as a company diplomat to smooth over client relations. Legend begs for you to play to his importance, but if he ever gets the impression you're putting him on display like some Westminster Kennel Club show dog, he might bite.

Don't completely discount Legend's penchant for mentoring and teaching. Legend might be willing to be assigned to an elite group of Futures, for example, where his tutelage might lead to some meaningful (read: credit-worthy) benefits to the company. Again, you need to finesse this, for if he views this as an "out to pasture" play, he'll discount the role and likely cause your Futures to wonder why they would ever want to achieve Legend status in your company. On the other hand, if you are able to successfully tout this as a mission-critical feature of company growth, then you might have found your vehicle for tapping Legend's deep contact list and institutional knowledge.

Disastrous Settings

Legend will hate you forever and make your life miserable if you take him out of his element and surround him with others who don't know or don't care about his stardom. Legend despises microman-agement, especially from some whippersnapper manager who has been with the company for a cup of coffee and now thinks he's Donald Trump. He doesn't want to attend every team meeting or training, but he doesn't want to be excluded either. You might want to present him with options and let him pick and choose.

Again, you need to avoid at all costs making Legend a show pony. He has no time for on-demand performances (imagine telling Jack Nicholson he had to sign autographs for four hours at some bullshit promotional appearance).

And, whatever you do, don't tell Legend he needs to change with the times ... ever!

Training/Coaching/Mentoring

Never, ever tell Legend that you're going to offer him some training. The very thought of getting training from someone like you is like-ly to send Legend into fits of uncontrollable laughter. And frankly, Legend doesn't need much training. Sure, he could brush up on some technology training, but do you really want to go there? (Do you remember the last time you got a call from your father—whom you love to pieces, and who's a wonderful father—asking for help accessing his e-mail. So you spent two hours unsuccessfully trying to help him resolve it? Right. Same thing with Legend—don't do it to yourself.)

Starting Five

STRATEGIES FOR MANAGING LEGEND

1   Treat Legend with kid gloves. You can't afford to lose this guy, and if he is half as successful as he acts like he is, then he probably could afford to leave if you piss him off.

2   Give him a part of the team meeting and training delivery. That will increase the likelihood that he actually shows up.

3   See if you can pair him with Future. He plainly won't be productive enough to justify his swollen pay, but if you can get him to transfer his knowledge and leverage some contacts, then you might make yourself even.

4   Put him in positions to shine and display his depth of industry know-how and connections.

Handling Miscues

By holding Legend to the same level of accountability as the others on your team, you are reminding him he is no longer your go-to guy. This must be done sparingly, and only in cases where harm is serious enough to warrant real discussion or action. Remember, Legend is a pro—albeit one past his prime—so the problems will be few and relatively benign. In other words, you can afford to tread lightly here.

Treat Legend like he is your rich grandfather who has stayed at the ballgame (or bar) a bit too long: get him off the bleachers, get him home, wash him up, and keep his dignity intact. He won't tell you to your face, but he'll remember what you did and he'll appreciate it.

What You Might Discuss with Legend

YOU: Legend, I was just curious. I sent you an e-mail the other day and haven't heard back from you.

LEGEND: Yeah, you know me, kid. I don't check my e-mail more than once a week. What was it about?

YOU: Well, I'm sort of stuck and I could use your help.

LEGEND: Really. A hotshot up-and-comer like you could use a little help from the old geezer? Amazing.

YOU: Um, right. Well, the truth is, the newbies on our team seem to be having some trouble managing some of their larger projects across divisions. My sense is that they would benefit from a little Legend training.

LEGEND: Look, kid. I'm old and tired, and I'm just trying to hang on until the end. I've got enough to worry about. Don't dump your problems on me.

YOU: You might be old, but you sure as hell are not tired. Look, I'm not looking to dump my problems on you. I'm at a loss here. Truthfully, we have some keepers there, but I don't think they'll make it if they keep falling on their faces like they have been. I think we have a chance to put in place a program to create a few more

(CONTINUED ON FOLLOWING PAGE)

Starting Five

(*CONTINUED*)

legends around here. I would do it if I could, but I haven't had any Legend training myself. I think there's a chance that we could use your training as a beta that, if successful, we could roll out across the department.

LEGEND: Hmm. That would be interesting. They could even roll that out company-wide.

YOU: Geez, I hadn't even thought of that. That would be unbelievable! What do you say?

LEGEND: Let me think about it.

YOU: Sure thing, but get back to me by week's end. I need to get moving on this. I've only gone to you about it, but I'll need to put something together regardless. I really want you to be the lead on this.

Character Combinations with Legend Worth Watching

- **FRANCHISE.** Legend was a Franchise. In fact, he probably was Franchise's mentor. In Legend's mind, he has never stopped being Franchise, so he may become competitive with Franchise unless the changing of the guard has occurred in broad daylight. This could make for some ugly team conflict, but could also result in fueling Legend to relive some of his glory days just to prove a point. And what manager wouldn't love that on their watch?

- **RETREAD.** Retread interviews, swaggers, and acts like Legend, but he has no past results to warrant such behavior. While Legend proudly, yet productively, begins to lose steam, Retread is an industry never-was. Legend will coolly and quickly identify Retread for the imposter that he is, and quickly poke holes in his embellished stories.

- **STEADY EDDIE.** All the below-the-radar qualities that make Eddie an asset might make for a nice comple-ment to Legend's sterling reputation. While Leg-end thinks PowerPoint is something that happens at a hockey game, Eddie has learned the intricacies that will help Legend freshen up his presentations and bring him into the twenty-first century. Putting these two together may very well increase Legend's production without threatening his kung fu grip on his contacts. And we know Eddie will be perfectly content being Tonto to Legend's Lone Ranger.

Keep or Throw Back?

Look, this guy can still deliver value. Legend at 60 percent of what he once was is better than just about anyone else you've got. No, he can't figure out how to use the "inter-web" and still can't envision why people would want phones "smarter" than they are. But he pos-sesses a library of institutional knowledge and industry know-how that, if tapped, could be extremely valuable to you.

You have to keep this guy. Moving him out, even if his decline becomes steadier, sends a poor message to others about how you might treat them if they deliver years of top performance. Plus, who the hell are you going to find to replace him? C'mon, you're doing whatever you can to keep Legend.

Character Profile #3

The Player

How Do You Know a Player When You See One?

You already know Player. He's the one hogging the mic on karaoke night. You hired him because he dazzled you. He does that to everyone. Man, Player is so smooth he makes plate glass look rough.

Player knows just what to say and how and when to say it. His cocktail party skills are unrivaled. He could fall into easy conversation with a tree stump.

Player has a knack for making people feel good. He wins over the guys in the copy room, so his jobs get handled first and with care. He enlivens what would otherwise be dreadful client engagements, so clients willingly attend them and remind themselves why they're doing business with your company in the first place. And when team morale is low, Player tends to say just the right thing to lift everyone's spirits and get them reengaged.

You'll see Player heaping praise on others—including you—but the praise comes so frequently and fervently as to eventually ring hollow. Indeed, Player celebrates others so those specific others will remember what a wonderful person Player is and respond in kind. But what do you know … his shit works.

The problem with Player is that subsequent impressions don't always match the dazzling first, and the longer you know Player the more he tends to reveal chinks in his armor.

Player is self-absorbed, absolutely loves the limelight, and is quietly vicious in his competition for others' affection. Player lacks depth, so once you get past the Yankees' playoff hopes and the weather, he might have little to offer you. At work, he's better at socializing than getting things done, but he's adept at getting others to do his bidding—and reaping the glory for himself. Player is often physically gifted—he's tall, beautiful, impeccably groomed, and dressed in colors that scream, "LOOK AT ME!" He's constantly flashing his broad smile, even when he's conspiring to toss you under the proverbial bus. Player speaks loudly and often while making sweeping hyperbolic claims about his own abilities.

THE PLAYERS

WHY YOU LOVE 'EM

- They bring high energy and enthusiasm all the time.

- They are exceptional schmoozers.

- They seek to be liked by all, and are often successful in their pursuit.

WHY YOU HATE 'EM

- They bring high energy and enthusiasm even when they're not wanted.

- They can come across like used car salesmen.

- Even a perceived slight by someone whose approval they're seeking can send them reeling.

Real-life/Screen Examples

- **Bill Clinton**—Slick Willy makes you feel like you're the center of his world when you're in his presence.

- **Ashton Kutcher**—can anyone be this happy this often?

- **Ryan Seacrest**—he hugs the Idolettes like they're blood relatives.

- **Kathy Lee Gifford**—her smile has been permanently plastered into her face…if only her brains were permanently plastered into her head.

A TRUE PLAYER: SLICK WILLY

It is commonly said about Bill Clinton that when you're in his presence, you feel as though you are the center of his universe. He makes you feel good—even if you're not a chubby intern in a stained blue dress. But as soon as he moves on to the next, and you're basking in the glow of the post-Willy ass pinch, he's forgotten everything about you.

Like Players everywhere, he possesses a level of charisma that mesmerizes and draws people to him. In his post-presidential days, he still packs a fund-raiser and works a room better than most active candidates. Bill seems addicted to outside attention, which is probably the only explanation for his nearly single-handedly derailing his wife's presidential campaign with his poorly timed public rants.

(CONTINUED ON FOLLOWING PAGE)

(CONTINUED)

His nearly insatiable appetite for women also evidences his Player tendencies—what better way to claim victory over someone's affections than sleeping with them?

Like most Players, Bill is also intensely thin-skinned. He struts confidently and seems steeped in self-assuredness, but behind this veil lays a deep reservoir of insecurity. Willy infamously turns purple-faced when an interviewer begins to cast him in unflattering light, and then usually manages to compose himself and conclude the interview with a series of passive-aggressive, condescending digs that are tantamount to sticking his tongue out and saying, "I was president and slept with the hot one from *Night Court* and you didn't!"

Ideal Settings

Player woos the hell out of people, so he thrives in settings that reward network-building and relationship brokering. Player uses his natural magnetism to draw in customers and business partners and win over unhappy clients, and is particularly good when his business relationships have a discreet beginning and end.

He is a huge hit at industry conferences, so be sure to have him manning the booth, emceeing big events, and especially hitting the after-parties. Player is especially skilled in environments that reward short-term exposure and superficial familiarity. Remember to consider natural laws of attrition: Player makes the dazzling first impression, and each subsequent impression is a little less dazzling than the one before it.

He also gets off on high visibility, access to influential people, and public recognition for success. He enjoys working in teams, and seems to feed off of others' energy and attention. Player gravitates toward rapidly changing environments, where no two days are quite alike. He absolutely abhors being told what to do and when, preferring instead to go wherever the wind takes him (which is usually somewhere in the vicinity of a stage, a microphone, and a camera).

Disastrous Settings

The very thought of working in predictable, detail-oriented jobs gives Player shingles, as does sitting among rows and rows of cubicle inhabitants. Being "one of the crowd" just ain't in his genetic makeup. This is your classic thirty-thousand-foot guy, so ask him to play in the weeds at your peril. Player tends to wear others down with his canned, shallow compliments and veiled criticisms, and his lack of depth will become problematic if he is exposed to subject-matter experts for any length of time. Contrary to his apparent rock-solid and confident exterior, Player is thin-skinned, so he will have particular trouble in openly hostile environments. Even sensitively delivered, constructive feedback can send him careening out of productivity for periods of time. To the extent straight cold-calling is required to generate sales, you might want to look beyond Player— the rejection associated with getting hung up on, or having doors slammed in his face, will be just too much for him to bear.

Training/Coaching/Monitoring

Flatter Player often, even if you don't really mean it. Player doesn't seek out the substance that tends to accompany your training, coaching and monitoring (he feels plenty confident that he knows it already), but he absolutely loves having you all to himself for any period of time, as well as having the opportunity to show off what he can do. Your biggest challenge when you're with him is getting past the façade and into what the hell he actually does all day. If you ask for detail and specifics about his activity, patterns, and accomplishments, he will try his mightiest to keep it vague and high-level. You might be better off just observing identifying patterns, and giving specific feedback about what you see. But remember, when giving constructive feedback, tread lightly. Though Player leads with confidence, he is fragile, and feedback delivered too harshly can send him on a "poor-me-my-boss-hates-me" binge for days. Find every opportunity to praise him. His fake humility will drive you to the edge, but it might build enough of a confidence cushion for you to deliver harsh news safely.

STRATEGIES FOR MANAGING PLAYER

If you don't have Player on your team already, you will (as you will be unable to resist him in the interview process—his specialty!). Therefore, you will need to know the following:

1	Whenever possible, vary Player's work responsibilities, scenery, and teammates.
2	Find creative ways to reward and recognize Player. It need not be huge financial bonuses. For example, an e-mail to upper management with a copy to Player recognizing Player's great work can go a long way.
3	Reward his good behavior with your attention. Player is needy, so reward him for good deeds when he's earned it.

4 If you must give Player a detail-driven task, be sure to have controls in place to audit his work. Remember, Player flies at thirty thousand feet—well above the weeds in which you just forced him to play!

5 Give Player the floor when you can. Let him lead a team meeting or make a big announcement. He's at his best when he has lots of eyes on him.

6 Watch out for backstabbing behavior from Player. He is often sneaky and competitive, and sometimes gets ahead by tearing others down behind their backs. Call him on it to let him know that you can see when he does it. He'll be shocked and appalled and insist he has no clue what you're talking about, but the behavior will diminish.

7 Be careful what you say and don't say to Player. He notoriously reads messages into words that were never intended by the sender. This has been exacerbated by the proliferation of e-mail! Single-word responses (e.g., "Okay") are interpreted by Player as some sign that you're mad at him. Because he tends to avoid direct conflict, you might only hear about it after you've seen his performance fall off a cliff.

8 Leverage his brokering skills. Player connects people well and he often has a vast network of people he knows just well enough. Because of his affinity for high-profile people, he might just be able to walk you into the C-suite of your hottest prospect.

9 Don't let him get bored. Player has a creative mind and can stir up some trouble when he's not occupied.

Starting Five

Handling Miscues

Player classically overstates his successes and downplays mistakes. So when you get a whiff that something is askew, you'll need to conduct your own independent investigation before approaching him. And no matter how glaring Player's offense, fight hard to lodge your criticism objectively and calmly, and well out of earshot of anyone else (they like attention but hate being publicly embarrassed). Once you state it, stay with him and help construct a correctional course that allows him to save face.

This serves two purposes. First, it helps put a plan in place right away that you crafted. Second, and perhaps more important, it sends a clear message to Player that you are not holding a grudge and you see a path to resolution so that you can put it behind you.

WHAT YOU MIGHT DISCUSS WITH PLAYER

PLAYER: Good morning, Boss! You look just beautiful this morning. Oh my God. I totally LOVE that sweater! It makes you look completely radiant!!

YOU: Thanks, Player. I like it too. How are you doing this morning?

PLAYER: I'm absolutely fabulous!! I just totally can't wait to get going today! I'm going to kill it. So many things to get done!

YOU: Great. Like what?

PLAYER: Oh, you know, just a lot of super-important things going on. I am going to dominate the industry today! Take the world by storm! Climb every mountain!

You: Cool. Just tell me about one thing you're going to do today. One concrete thing.

Player: Oh, I'm having lunch with the chairman of Pepsi today. I just know our firm was meant to do business with them, and he's going to hear me out on why I feel that way. After that I need to shoot across town for coffee with the mayor and his chief of staff to convince them to okay our client's free public concert series.... Oops! Gotta run! Steady Eddie needs my help pulling a proposal together. He's so cute, the way he hems and haws before actually doing anything. That sweet little thing just sometimes needs a nudge. See ya, Boss! I love ya!

Character Combinations with Player Worth Watching

- **SLACKER.** Slacker is basically a poor man's version of Player. He is neither as attractive nor as popular, so his limited depth is construed as an outcrop of his own laziness, not charming aloofness. Also, Slacker's motivation is different from Player's. Slacker looks for corners to cut to make his life easier without you noticing. Player looks to please everyone, so he bites off more than he can chew and, as a result, drops the ball and misses important details.

- **NEEDY NED.** Ned and Player can complement each other nicely. Ned seeks attention through whining and neediness by leading with low self-esteem, while Player seeks attention by confidently talking loudly and boldly predicting greatness. Ned's neediness alone will win Player's initial attention, but Ned will have to lead with his awe for Player if he wants to keep it. And doing so might prove fruitful. Player would benefit from Ned's attention to detail, and Ned would benefit from the doors Player could open.

- **OTHER PLAYERS.** Bored and in need of some reality TV-styled entertainment? Tell Player #1 and Player #2 that you are thinking of sending just one of them to be interviewed by a local TV station. Then sit back and enjoy the backstabbing, attention-grabbing duel of a lifetime.

Keep or Throw Back?

As with anyone of these characters, if Player is in the right environment, he tends to do well. By virtue of his being charismatic, confident, and initially appealing, he is likely to find some measure of success. But if you rely heavily on deep knowledge, detail, and accountability, he might not make it.

Character Profile #4

The Badass

How Do You Know a Badass When You See One?

You know a Badass when you meet one because she shoves her Badassness in your face. She's brash and cocky and bold. She reeks of an absolute self-assuredness that states clearly her intention to one day rule the world. This self-starter oozes confidence in a way that turns many people off—including certain clients and prospects—immediately.

Badass produces. A lot. She succeeds because she is constantly moving forward, with absolutely no regard for restraint or delicacy or boundaries. Badass is never afraid of hearing "No!"—she actually might be immune to it—and eagerly awaits assignment of the next task.

She's a true business predator and hunts for weaker prey she can bend into submission to do her bidding and help her achieve her goals. Her attention to detail is miserable, but her activity level is off the charts.

The Badass is just as likely to run over colleagues as she is anyone else, and so you'll often find yourself picking people up off the floor in her wake.

Starting Five

She interrupts others, is prone to shouting, refuses to share helpful information or team resources, and will ignore team norms, customs, and rules if she thinks they're stupid. This is the woman who barges into your one-on-one with another employee only to scream about the incompetency of an entire department. Badass walks quickly, talks loudly, and always speaks in the same abrasive tone to everyone she encounters. Think fingernails on a chalkboard.

Want to see the Badass sit still for a minute? Hand her the latest employee evaluations and divisional rankings at the next team meeting. She's as competitive as they come, and will stop at nothing until she is numero uno. Badass doesn't need praise or hand-holding…she just needs to know who and where the competition is and what it will take to beat them. Teams, uniforms, and affiliations mean nothing to her. Badass is one woman against the world.

THE BADASSES

WHY YOU LOVE 'EM	WHY YOU HATE 'EM
• They work their asses off.	• They leave bodies in their wake.
• They don't require much of your time.	• They ignore your advice, even when you know it would help them.
• You don't have to keep tabs on their activity… they are always working.	• Their flexible ethics could land you in a heap of shit.

Real-life/Screen Examples

- **Demi Moore**—bold, take-no-shit G.I. Jane…yet Ashton always kept smiling…hmmm.

- **Dick Cheney**—has never minced a word in his life.

- **Angelina Jolie**—back off, Jenny…I want me some Brad.

- **Dwight Schrute from *The Office***—Number one at Dunder Mifflin every bleeping month.

- **Hillary Clinton**—struts into the Kremlin in her pantsuit and tells Putin where he can shove it.

- **Martha Stewart**—if you cross her, she'll rip your heart out and then turn it into a Christmas ornament.

- **Gregory House, MD, from *House***—even with a cane, this guy is a Badass.

ONE BADASS: DWIGHT SCHRUTE

Ever watch *The Office* on NBC? Dwight Schrute is Dunder Mifflin's pet Badass. He assumes informal positions of authority—he always refers to himself as Assistant Regional Manager, only to be corrected by his boss, Michael Scott, that he is officially Assistant *to* the Regional Manager—as if they're granted by divine intervention. He unemotionally imposes his will on customers and colleagues. He takes whatever he wants—without concern for anyone but himself (Exhibit A: Angela, the uptight accountant whom Dwight was regularly sleeping with throughout her engagement to their Cornell alum colleague, Andy).

(CONTINUED ON FOLLOWING PAGE)

(*CONTINUED*)

He couldn't care less about being liked, and cares entirely about being the best. He also happens to consistently be the best damned sales rep in the Scranton office.

You want some real insight into the mind of a Badass? Watch Dwight when Michael Scott is temporarily unseated as branch manager. Dwight seizes command as if he were a military dictator.

Note: Dwight is also blessed with some Whistler tendencies, which only add to others' disdain for him. He rats out (or maces) anyone committing even the most minor infraction. While these behaviors typically fall outside Badass behavior, Dwight whistles to curry favor with management, assert his authority over colleagues, and improve his own stature in the company—objectives entirely consistent with those of Badasses everywhere.

Ideal Settings

Badass brings a lot to the table, and her confidence and inner drive to succeed make her a success almost anywhere she goes, particularly when her objectives are clearly defined and the rewards for meeting them are great. Therefore, Badass tends to outperform if:

1. Her job description and your expectations are clear;
2. She is publicly ranked against her peers; and
3. She's left alone to work every day with her favorite person (herself) to find a successful path and deliver results.

Badass thrives in pressure-filled, time-sensitive tasks, as her unwavering confidence keeps her from losing sight of the ultimate objective. Mind you, while Badass remains confident under pressure, she doesn't remain calm. She can inflict serious harm during her raging fits, so do watch for casualties. Finally, Badass loves to act alone, in her own way, and without dependence on anyone else. When she alone stands to gain glory or shame, she'll thrive and gain as much glory as anyone is willing to give her.

Disastrous Settings

Badass does not do well in positions devoid of clearly defined objectives or measures of success, or when she's forced to rely too heavily on others. In these environments, Badass tends to get abusive toward her peers, and often winds up across from her HR rep defending her bad actions.

The standard nine-to-five office job tends to be the scene of most Badass implosions. She just doesn't jive with the punch-the-clock folks. And because these environments rely on predictable, steady, and cooperative behavior, they tend to weed out Badass even before Badass can reject them.

She doesn't do well in team meetings or think-tank environments either. Badass is a driven achiever, one who is only at peace when she's in full motion and on the brink of taking over the world.

Training/Coaching/Monitoring

You will see many developmental opportunities for Badass, and you might well be inclined to move in aggressively and tweak this producer in an attempt to maintain her performance while adding some personality and sensitivity. Also, Badass will insist on doing everything her way, even if it's less efficient than your way. But before you intervene, weigh the costs and benefits. If Badass thinks you're riding her too hard, she might react negatively to the point where you might risk losing her. ("You're giving me feedback?! What about those other effing losers? If I were you, that's where I'd be spending my management energy.") Even if your intervention doesn't escalate Badass's temper, she's likely to simply ignore your message and continue on as she always does. That's not to say that you need to treat Badass gingerly. We just want you to think about the return on your time and energy. You want a reason to monitor and coach Badass? Wait until you see a slip in performance. Badass is concrete, and she expects her boss to lean on her if she's falling short of company expectations. In those moments, see if you can get Badass to identify what's going wrong and enlist her to develop her own plan to close the gap. Because even when Badass is open to your management focus, she's more likely to embrace an idea she deems her own.

STRATEGIES FOR MANAGING THE BADASS

Managing Badass can be a handful, but you will find success by keeping the following in mind:

1	Set crystal-clear goals and objectives, and make sure they're difficult (but possible) to achieve.
2	Pit her in a contest against someone—even herself—and constantly and publicly show Badass her ranking. She'll fight like hell to win.
3	Give her some time and space to figure out her own way of doing things (even if you know a better way, she'll ignore it, which will only piss you off).

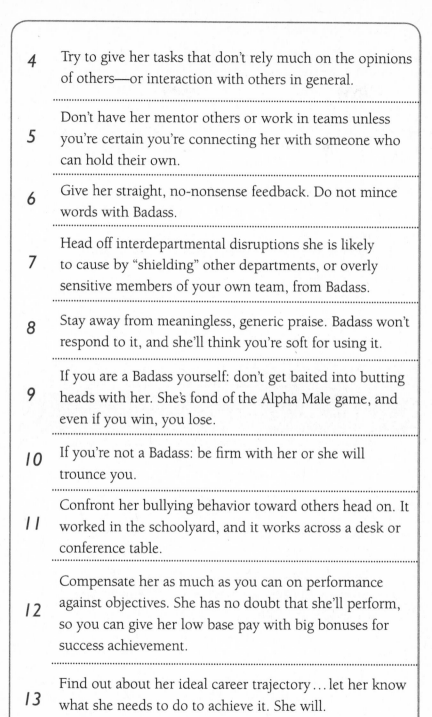

4   Try to give her tasks that don't rely much on the opinions of others—or interaction with others in general.

5   Don't have her mentor others or work in teams unless you're certain you're connecting her with someone who can hold their own.

6   Give her straight, no-nonsense feedback. Do not mince words with Badass.

7   Head off interdepartmental disruptions she is likely to cause by "shielding" other departments, or overly sensitive members of your own team, from Badass.

8   Stay away from meaningless, generic praise. Badass won't respond to it, and she'll think you're soft for using it.

9   If you are a Badass yourself: don't get baited into butting heads with her. She's fond of the Alpha Male game, and even if you win, you lose.

10   If you're not a Badass: be firm with her or she will trounce you.

11   Confront her bullying behavior toward others head on. It worked in the schoolyard, and it works across a desk or conference table.

12   Compensate her as much as you can on performance against objectives. She has no doubt that she'll perform, so you can give her low base pay with big bonuses for success achievement.

13   Find out about her ideal career trajectory...let her know what she needs to do to achieve it. She will.

Handling Miscues

Badass is a lightning rod for controversy, and she often finds herself in hot water with rival departments, upper management, and difficult clients. You need to be very clear in your own mind about your policies here. How much shit are you willing to live with from one of your consistent producers? Are you willing to stick your neck out for her? Are you willing to see her leave if she feels you don't have her back? Once your policies are crystal clear to you and everyone else (including Badass), you can respond accordingly. If Badass crosses the line and violates your policy, then you meet her head on. Don't beat around the bush. Don't apologize for inconveniences. Don't tell her what a valued employee she is. Identify the behavior and state what the consequences are. Get Badass to recognize her own contribution to the problem and then help her identify how she's going to make it better. Badass can take your tough love. Believe us.

WHAT YOU MIGHT DISCUSS WITH BADASS

You: Um, Badass, you got a minute?

Badass: This better be good, Boss. I've got things to do.

You: Yeah, well, I got a call from my counterpart in marketing. Seems your little tirade in their department yesterday has prompted them to postpone their marketing plan on your new product design until you and I sit down with the marketing associates you tortured, along with their manager. Way to go.

Badass: What?! They're complete idiots! I design ingenious products. They're supposed to market them.

You: According to their manager, they think you're the idiot. We need to get this behind us or you're going to find yourself with no one willing to bring your products to market. I'd hate to see your ingenuity fail to hit the production line.

Badass: But!...

You: Listen, for better or worse, my fate rests in your hands. So I want you to get your products to market as much as you do. Even though we have different methods of achieving our goals, we do have the same interests. Let's come up with a strategy for getting out of this meeting with them thinking you're sorry—even if you're not—so they can revisit their position. In the meantime, you and I can hammer out a process to avoid these issues between you and them in the future.

Character Combinations with Badass Worth Watching

- **THE FUTURE.** Future might find Badass alluring, what with Badass's undying work ethic and ability to post gaudy numbers every month. But be concerned if you see Future opting for Badass's company over, say, that of Legend or Franchise. You've already put out plenty of fires on Badass's behalf. Yes, you want Future to produce, but you want her doing so in a way that makes your life easier, not harder.

- **THE NOODLER.** Want to see something funny? Watch Badass in your next team meeting when Noodler holds everyone up to share his research on the market impact of seventeen-year locusts. Badass begins by rolling her eyes and tapping her toes. Fifteen minutes in, she blows a gasket. Noodler's obsessive-compulsive tendencies don't mesh with Badass's impulsivity and inattention to detail. These two won't get each other, and neither will care. Just sit back and enjoy the show.

- **STEADY EDDIE.** Watch Steady Eddie's lips quiver when Badass calls him a "stammering retard" after Steady Eddie nervously asks about the "p-p-pending p-p-product-line changes." Badass is a pit bull who attacks when she smells fear. Your concern is whether Steady Eddie can continue delivering stable performance when he's constantly watching his back for signs of Badass. Badass's ability to drive Steady Eddie to learned helplessness is the main reason to minimize interaction between the two.

Keep or Throw Back?

If you can tolerate Badass's insensitivities while not getting run over by her, you'll keep her because she produces. Note: Please watch to make sure she's not running over your other people while you're not looking. Her productivity aside, if she chases off others or adversely impacts their performance, the costs of keeping her might exceed the benefits.

Character Profile #5

The Future

How Do You Know a Future You See One?

"Did he just call me a 'Noob'?" you ask incredulously. "Find out what he is talking about and tell him to come fix my computer again." Ah...Future enters the workplace, making us all feel old. He was born when you were in high school. Make a *Breakfast Club* reference and Future is lost. Pearl Jam is "old school" and *Old School* is a classic "old" movie. What happened?

In spite of his propensity to annoy us with his boldness, brashness, naiveté (which can cost you dearly), and youth, Future reminds you of, well, you. He walks with the same swagger, confidently pursues ladies far beyond his level, and is as comfortable talking with a CEO as he is a college buddy.

Future is most notable for his sheer raw talent. He's far from polished, and makes plenty of mistakes, but he leads with confidence, demonstrates undeniable promise at nearly every turn, and acquires knowledge and skill at an eye-popping rate. He's so good so early that Future gets praise from Day One, and comes to think of himself as the second coming of Franchise.

Future is smart and tireless, but his eyes have a tendency to wander. Your biggest challenge with Future is keeping him satisfied that the training wheels you've now got strapped to him will be shed soon, and that opportunity to achieve his inevitable stardom will come shortly. The good news is that you'll always know where he stands—he doesn't yet have a hold on workplace norms, so he won't know that he should withhold from you information about his ongoing job search.

THE FUTURES

WHY YOU LOVE 'EM

- They're packed with upside. They're good now, but you know that they will only get better with time.

- They are self-motivated, hungry to learn, and absorb like sponges. It's like teaching a new language to kindergartners.

- They will make you look like Super Manager because they'll perform well right out of the gate.

WHY YOU HATE 'EM

- It's always a threat that they'll leave you for someone else who spots their potential and offers them a quicker path to greatness.

- They think they know a lot more than they do, so they ignore the lessons you want to teach them.

- They'll promote themselves endlessly and happily nudge you out of the way to report to the senior execs just what studs they are.

Real-life/Screen Examples

- **Tim Lincecum**—known as "the Freak," this World Series-winning pitcher takes on perennial all-stars with his small stature and unorthodox delivery.

- **Doogie Howser, MD**—this TV show doctor—a mere sixteen-year-old—is a classic Future.

- **Tiger Woods, circa 1996**—was there any tournament he thought he wouldn't win?

- **Michelle Wie**—this pro golfer played with the men…before she even beat the women.

FACEBOOK'S FUTURE: MARK ZUCKERBERG

Okay, this kid launches Facebook from his Harvard dorm room in 2004, based on an idea he began developing in *high school*. He and a couple of college buddies decided to head to Silicon Valley and seek investment money, and the next thing he knew, Mark Zuckerberg was one of the youngest billionaires on the planet.

Since its inception, Facebook has revolutionized how people interact online, and presently boasts more than 500 million active users. Many commentators wonder whether Zuckerberg will ever return to Harvard to complete his degree. We can almost hear Zuckerberg, a Future through and through, snickering and commenting to himself: "College? Who the hell needs college? I'm a friggin' billionaire and I'm not even thirty years old!"

Authors' Note: Sean and John are personally indebted to Mr. Zuckerberg, for without Facebook, we would not likely have reconnected and we would never have come together to write this book.

Ideal Settings

It's no mystery what drives Future: accomplishment and perpetual proof of his worth and intelligence to you, him, and all those around him. He will want to do more, earn more, and get promoted faster than anyone in the company's history. So Future thrives in environments rich in individual achievement and recognition, and one that does not give much weight to tenure when determining promotion or assignment of responsibility.

Also keep in mind that instead of trying to build a better mousetrap, Future would probably rather find a way to genetically alter the mouse to stay out of the kitchen in the first place. His creativity and innovative nature is virtually limitless, so finding ways to perpetually challenge your young charge will take you a long way toward achieving your goals and keeping Future around to achieve his.

Disastrous Settings

Future feels imprisoned by environments that rely too heavily on tenure and precedent, so rigidly hierarchical structures that call for strict reporting lines will send Future digging for a quick escape. You would also be wise to avoid giving Future mind-numbing, mundane tasks that you typically dole out to run-of-the-mill newbies. Large law firms that promote and administer raises based solely on tenure (when you begin, you're a first-year with all other first-years; and the next year you're a second-year with all other second-years, and so on) are the classic anti-Future environments. Future deserves to shine and stand out from the herd, so environments that don't permit that will be sure to lose him.

Perhaps more important than formal promotions and raises, however, might be work variety and level of responsibility. Hide Future from clients, keep him off the company's coolest projects, and enlist him in the same old shit day in and day out, and Future will be running for the doors.

Training/Coaching/Monitoring

Give lots of thought to how you're going to train and coach Future. The leadership gurus tell you that every new hire is an identical block of clay that, with the requisite care and attention (and hugs) from you, they will achieve their true potential, and all of you will join hands and sing the company fight song at the annual picnic. But we all know that not all newbies are created equal, and Future is the finest damn block of clay you've ever seen. This block of clay requires special handling, more frequent touches, with exhibition at the Guggenheim being the end goal. Make sure Future spends time with company executives, Franchise, and other well-regarded new hires across the company. You want him internalizing the best qualities and habits of the very best around.

Also, because you are paranoid of losing Future, be sure to spend time understanding his hopes and aspirations so you can shape his experience and help him realize them. Look, Future has the potential to become your next Franchise. You want to know what makes him tick so you can keep him happy and productive, and help him realize his greatness. So who cares if it's just the two of you singing the fight song at the company picnic? Future is probably the only one worth singing with anyway.

> *We all know that not all newbies are created equal, and Future is the finest damn block of clay you've ever seen. This block of clay requires special handling, more frequent touches, with exhibition at the Guggenheim being the end goal.*

Starting Five

STRATEGIES FOR MANAGING FUTURE

1	Meet with Future early and often so you can head off concerns, shape his development, and learn his hopes and dreams.
2	Keep Future in the company of the best and brightest you've got—you want the good shit rubbing off on him.
3	Find ways to feed Future added responsibility and show him a viable, near-term path to promotion.
4	Address ugly habits early.
5	Keep work product varied, so Future doesn't get bored and restless.
6	Where appropriate, introduce Future to upper management to give him exposure.
7	Make it clear to Future that you have high hopes for him, and that you are taking concrete steps to help Future achieve them. The more Future knows you're working for him and that you believe in him, the less likely it is that he'll look to move.

Handling Miscues

Oh, with Future there will be miscues. A rookie of the year gets caught with drugs. The young R&B star dubbed the "next Michael Jackson" beats up his equally famous girlfriend. Having talent and brains does not change the fact that a twenty-four-year-old is still twenty-four years old. Errors, egregious or otherwise, are to be expected and treated with two things in mind:

1. You do not want them to happen again.
2. You do not want constant correction to cause you and Future to shift your focus from his pending greatness to his company rap sheet.

There's a sliding scale here. The first few offenses warrant kid glove treatment. After all, you don't want to scare the kid off by getting him thinking that he's dug himself a hole that he'll never be able to get out of. But if the mistakes continue, you'll need to step up the consequences and monitoring. After all, the kid only shows promise at this point, and has certainly not earned Franchise treatment. Not only will you send the wrong message to Future, but you're likely to raise hell among the other schmucks who routinely find themselves in your doghouse for the same behavior.

What You Might Discuss with Future

You: Future, how are you making out with those projections?

Future: I finished those an hour after you asked me for them. I just handed them off to my assistant to review. We should have them back to you shortly.

You: Wow! An hour? Impressive. Wait, you have an assistant? And what have you been doing while he's reviewing them?

Future: Well, I didn't like the way they turned out, so I decided to call down to marketing and ask them to send me four more reports so I could start to figure out where the extra expenses were originating from. I found a glitch in the system.

You: You did?

Future: Yes. But while I was rewriting the software, I hit a "Fatal Error" and got a blue screen, so now I have a call into the developer, who is in Portugal. So it looks like we are down for the rest of the day. Maybe tomorrow, too.

You: Huh? The rest of the day?

Future: Yes, sorry, Boss. Oh, and I was running late this morning, so I parked in the CFO's spot while he was about to pull into it. And while I was walking into the office he had something to say about it…just a heads up.

Character Combinations with Future Worth Watching

- **FRANCHISE.** Connect Future with Franchise as soon as possible. Let Franchise's professionalism, success, and responsible nature be passed along from the first day of Future's employment. Let Future know that Franchise is the gold standard and see if you can't connive Franchise into taking Future under his wing. Success is contagious.

- **MR. INAPPROPRIATE.** Future is going to find Mr. I hilarious. Why wouldn't he? Everyone except Whistler does. Unfortunately, Future is not far removed from fraternity row, and if you're not careful, Mr. I's office will turn into Delta House, and the Belushi in him will zero in on Future as his new pledge. Try to minimize Future's unmonitored exposure to Mr. I, and spend a little time convincing Future that Mr. I's ways are a thing of the past and likely to limit Mr. I's upward mobility. Future's ambitions should be enough of a safety mechanism to keep him from farting in the break room.

- **SLACKER.** Here comes Slacker rearing his ugly head again. He's looking for partners in crime and takes particular pleasure in scoring the major coup. And what coup is more major than coaxing Future—Boss's pet—over to the dark side. Look out…this one has some catastrophic consequences.

Keep or Throw Back?

Good managers live to get their hands on a Future. If you throw him back, pack it in and resign.

Character Profile #6

Steady Eddie

How Do You Know a Steady Eddie When You See One?

Steady Eddie is the glue that keeps a team together. The problem is that he's also classically invisible, rigidly adherent to process and roles, and as quiet as a church mouse. He does all the dreadful behind-the-scenes shit that no one else likes to do. And because he runs from attention, he avoids taking credit even when he deserves it.

If Steady Eddie were a basketball player, he would be the guy passing to the guys who get the assists ... or deflecting a missed shot into the hands of a teammate so the teammate gets the rebound ... and then helping a teammate off the floor after he was knocked down. People often ignore Steady Eddie (because he's so easy to ignore) and fail to see his value until he's long gone.

Eddie leads with his insecurity, and questions himself every step of the way, which can be especially annoying to you, a self-assured manager. And Eddie speaks so damned quietly you'll constantly find yourself asking him to repeat what he just said.

STEADY EDDIES

WHY YOU LOVE 'EM	WHY YOU HATE 'EM
• They do the shit no one else wants to do.	• They do a lot of useless shit (or at least shit that isn't measureable).
• They'll hit singles all day long.	• All they do is hit singles.
• They'll let you know when someone on your team is hurting.	• They're basketcases immobilized by their own awareness of interpersonal dynamics.

Real-life/Screen Examples

- **Alice from *The Brady Bunch***—the secret sauce that held that crazy Brady household together.
- **All NFL Right Tackles**—*The Blind Side* gave their left tackle counterparts all the fanfare, but these right-side guys have to protect the QB as well.
- **Shane Battier**—NBA's king of intangibles.
- **Yo, Adriane! (Rocky's wife)**—could the Rock have beaten Mr. T without Adrian there to tearfully will him to victory?

FOOTBALL'S STEADY EDDIES: NFL RIGHT TACKLES

Since *The Blind Side* became a hit book and movie, America has learned a lot about NFL left tackles. Left tackles like Michael Oher and D'Brickashaw Ferguson, although not quite household names like Brett Favre and Terrell Owens, are slowly making their way into the celebrity ranks. But how many *right* tackles can you name? Yeah, that's what we thought.

These guys and their equally anonymous defensive tackle counterparts blend into a football game like massive, turf-camouflaged elephants. Most casual fans look right past them. Right tackles are your classic blue-collar, role-playing, attention-deflecting football players, whose value is not truly appreciated until they get beaten badly on a play, which results in their running back (for whom they were trying to create a hole) getting his teeth bashed in by a hulking linebacker.

Right tackles seem to exist solely to catapult their team's star-studded roster into the limelight. They don't seek fame or fortune, or even a uniform that makes them look slimmer. They just want to do their damn job and help their team win. So every single play, they break from huddle, get in their stance, and do their job. No flash. Nothing brilliant. Nothing catastrophic. Just steady, consistent performers.

Ideal Settings

Eddie thrives in stable, predictable, team-centric work environments, particularly when his strengths are leveraged and palpably appreciated. Opportunities with crystal-clear roles and processes (or uncertain and broken ones that Eddie is enlisted to clarify and fix) bring out the very best in Steady Eddie.

Eddie likes being part of a "work family." Indeed, he constantly does little things behind the scenes to create one. Eddie quietly picks someone up when they seem down, discretely alerts the boss (i.e., you) about destructive tensions that exist on the team, anonymously brings a tray of homemade brownies to the weekly team meeting, and sends a warm, handwritten note recognizing someone else's achievement. Eddie is commonly found in customer service departments or on pre-sales teams but has the potential to blossom in almost every environment, provided there are people there able to recognize his value.

Disastrous Settings

A self-starter he is not. Rapidly changing, unpredictable work settings that require participants to frequently assert themselves and don numerous hats are Steady Eddie's worst nightmare.

Does your team need to be able to change direction on a dime? Do your policies vary by prospect and client? If so, your Eddie will easily unravel.

Also, don't be surprised to find Eddie racing from cutthroat situations that only recognize individual achievement. Steady Eddie tends to get run over and bullied in these environments, and whatever contribution he might make is completely unappreciated. Eddie often needs his hand held, especially in environments void of clarity and predictability.

Training/Coaching/Monitoring

Steady Eddie absolutely loves training, coaching, and monitoring. Indeed, he can often be found wallowing in it. See, the thing is that he needs to know "the steps," and training sessions might be the only place he can get them. Eddie is the one who combs through the instruction manual when he gets a new computer and sets it up step by step, while the rest of the world turns it on and learns by doing. Eddie approaches everything the very same way. He's a nut about routines and habit.

> *He might get paralyzed because he thinks he doesn't know enough, even when you know he does. But once he's on his way, you won't need to do much monitoring of Eddie.*

When you're managing Eddie, you need to be sensitive of his need for clearly laid-out processes. You might not think you have a clear process for doing things because you act on gut instinct, but see if you can articulate various processes you have adapted for conducting business and write down the steps. Believe it or not, that document will become Eddie's bible and will cut his heart rate in half. Don't want to go through that trouble? Try this: have Eddie shadow Franchise for a day and write down his take on Franchise's processes; go over them with him during your next one-on-one. You'll also want to make sure you nudge him into motion. He might get paralyzed because he thinks he doesn't know enough, even when you know he does. But once he's on his way, you won't need to do much monitoring of Eddie, because he'll be as predictable as can be. You'll come to know that promptly at noon every Tuesday he eats two slices of pepperoni pizza at the joint on the corner of Main and Spruce.

STRATEGIES FOR MANAGING STEADY EDDIE

Managing Steady Eddie can be maddening, particularly if you are a Badass or a Player (or anyone else who tends to prefer action over deliberation). This guy can drive you nuts. So here are some suggestions for getting more from him without driving yourself off the deep end:

1	Precisely because Eddie is so inclined to help with even the most undesirable of tasks, you can find creative ways to play to his strengths in a manner that actually helps you.
2	Enlist him to research, identify, and fix a broken process.
3	Tap Eddie for his insights into team morale and intra-team tensions to head off bigger problems.
4	If you live in a world of rapid and unpredictable change, help Eddie create his own processes for anticipating and handling change when it arrives. You will put him at ease, but more importantly, get substantially more productivity and effectiveness out of him.
5	Finally, please do step in if Eddie is getting bullied. As we mentioned, his value is often not fully realized until he's gone, and if he gets bullied enough without intervention from you or someone else, he will be gone very soon. One of the worst things that can happen to any manager is to have a key role player or two depart. Eddie is very hard to replace!

Handling Miscues

More likely than not, you'll learn of Eddie's miscues from Eddie before you hear it from any other source. Steady Eddie owns his shit better than you or anyone else. The only concern is that he overreacts to his mistakes and beats himself up over them. When he comes to you in tears apologizing for ruining the company, invite Eddie into your office, help him pull himself together, and get the whole story from him (even though he'll tell it to you in far more detail than you'll ever need). Once you have all the details, you can objectively assess the damage, and then you and Eddie can pull together a very detailed process to clear his conscience and get him back on track.

WHAT YOU MIGHT DISCUSS WITH STEADY EDDIE

YOU: Eddie, so nice to see you. Feels like we haven't crossed paths in some time. Where have you been? What have you been up to lately?

EDDIE: (Something quiet and unintelligible.)

YOU: What? Can you say that again? I didn't hear anything you said.

EDDIE: Oh, okay, sorry, Boss...I said I've been up to a bunch of stuff—helping Player organize and rehearse his presentation for the national conference, assisting Legend with his online training (you know, he's still a bit uncomfortable with anything "virtual"), and getting Future up to speed on the industry players in our market.

(CONTINUED ON FOLLOWING PAGE)

Utility Players

(CONTINUED)

You: That's great. I'm sure they all appreciate it. But I'm curious about how you're managing to get your own stuff done.

Eddie: Well, you know me, Boss. I usually manage to fit my stuff in between everything else. I get in at 6:30 a.m., review my calendar and plan my day while I have half a cup of coffee and my morning yogurt, and send out reminder e-mails to the team about upcoming deadlines they're facing. Between 7 a.m. and 8 a.m. I catch up on paperwork. At 8 a.m. I meet with Slacker in the cafeteria (it's that little agreement you and I have to get him here in the morning on time). By 8:30 a.m....

You: ...Okay, I get the idea. I know you have your rituals, and that's fine. And all you offer our team is good for everyone. I guess what I'm concerned about is how much time you're spending on things outside your actual job description. That might explain why your reviews fall squarely in the consistently average range.

Eddie: Boss, if someone needs me, I help them. It's just the way I am.

Character Combinations with Eddie Worth Watching

- **THE BADASS.** This is likely to be an abusive relationship. Eddie knows all the rote and boring information that Badass is too busy to learn. And as Eddie starts to slowly teach Badass the correct way to fill out paperwork and adhere to rules, Badass may actually help put a little bass in Eddie's voice and get him some of the respect he deserves. But beware— unmonitored time with Badass and Eddie can lead to many tissues and HR visits. An unchecked Badass is likely to run roughshod over a defenseless Eddie.

- **THE PLAYER.** Allowing Player to "play" his game, with Eddie in the background doing the real work, may create a team that is Franchise-esque in its production. Player kicks open doors with his charm, and Eddie walks through, holds the client's hand, manages all the details, and makes the client feel like she is part of the family. Player will sing (literally) Eddie's praises, and the two just might make a decent team.

- **ADHD BUTTERFLY.** There is probably no other character quite as maddening to Eddie as Butterfly. Butterfly's sheer unpredictability and complete disregard for convention and workplace norms give Eddie hives. And Eddie's pleas for order and process will send Butterfly fluttering away to someone who cares about order a whole lot less.

Keep or Throw Back?

If Eddie can't hack the pace of change or cutthroat nature of your workplace, then he will self-select out if it's early on in his tenure; once he gets some tenure behind him, he won't.

Whether you keep Eddie or kick him to the curb will hinge on the Eddie's ability to find a role that enables him to contribute meaningfully and find (or build in) routine and predictability in his world.

Character Profile #7

The Noodler

How Do You Know a Noodler When You See One?

Just about every work team everywhere has a Noodler. At first blush, Noodler seems to exist for no other reason than to make us all crazy. But Noodler considers his purpose much nobler than that. In his own mind, Noodler exists to clean up the mess you boobs create on a daily basis; he does this by providing exhaustive research to back up (or refute) your bold claims, and to bring back to earth (or completely obliterate) your silly thirty-thousand-foot fantasies.

At team meetings, Noodler holds everyone up by asking "why" every five minutes, and by using the Socratic method to poke holes in loosely reached conclusions one question at a time. Others will shuffle papers, roll their eyes, and shift restlessly in their seats to signal that they're losing patience with Noodler, but their efforts are lost on him. He is always the smartest guy in the room...just ask him.

Noodler can find the answers to every question...just give him enough time and resources. Just don't ask him to move too quickly, deliver in bullet points, or meet hard deadlines. Noodler's fastest gear is plodding, and his briefest presentation is encyclopedic. He will take a problem, turn it on its head, and then add four layers of complexity. Noodler is likely to lose ground to faster-moving colleagues who deliver clean, crisp proposals (as compared with Noodler's bulky, hardbound versions).

To make managing him more interesting, Noodler tends toward the curmudgeonly, so don't expect warm fuzzies from him. He will hit you square between the eyes with the truth (or at least his version of it), and if you openly disagree with him, you better have some facts to back up your position, or he will drag your team meeting on even further.

THE NOODLERS

WHY YOU LOVE 'EM

- They spend time turning over stones that can uncover something that can save your ass.

- They deliver impeccable paperwork and detailed reports.

- They often ask the tough questions that help your team flesh out a proposed plan.

WHY YOU HATE 'EM

- They spend time turning over stones that uncover nothing other than your suppressed rage for him.

- Their paperwork is usually late and is laden with information for which you have no use.

- They are annoying naysayers that bring down your spirits when an uplifting idea is put forth.

Real-life/Screen Examples

- **Bill Belichick (head coach of New England Patriots)**—Belli-Cheat (as New York Jet fans call him) pours over hours of (illegally obtained) film every week.

- **The Professor from *Gilligan's Island***—transforming coconuts into transmitters.

- **Your Mother (when you were 17 and tried to borrow the car to go out on a Saturday night)**—C'mon, Mom, I don't need to hear anymore teenage DWI statistics!

THE ULTIMATE NOODLER: MOM

You love her now, but you spent your teen years despising her. She could spot a hole in your sock buried deep under a pile of laundry and smell a pack of cigarettes in the basement closet. She spent hours combing through your homework assignments, identifying every dangling participle and making you rewrite the whole damned thing. And even when Dad gave the okay for you to attend the make-out party around the way, Mom came up with fifteen reasons why you shouldn't, couldn't, and wouldn't. Mom always knew best...just ask her.

Utility Players

Ideal Settings

With Noodler, you get the best bang for your buck when he is in a role that demands and rewards high attention to detail and quality over quantity. Lawyers and accountants are your quintessential Noodlers because their clients depend on them to get it 100 percent right the first time. Noodler can succeed in a deadline-driven environment (think print editor at a major daily newspaper), but only if he's part of a team led by someone who recognizes Noodler's strengths, gives him plenty of lead time, tightly controls the amount of shit on his plate, and tolerates Noodler's endless whininess. Noodler likes to take his knowledge out for a spin and to hear the world tell him how damn smart he is, so be sure to stroke the intellectual ego that lies deep within.

Disastrous Settings

Like Steady Eddie, don't expect Noodler to create anything out of thin air. He doesn't kick up dust...Noodler settles dust at an excruciatingly slow pace. Loosely structured outside sales environments, in which reps are expected to generate their own leads, nurture them through a sales process, and ultimately close them are likely to crush Noodler. He's not really a people person, so he can have a hard time connecting with those who might ultimately drive business his way. In addition, Noodler is likely to lock onto a small handful of prospects rather than have an active pipeline of countless ones.

With Noodler, the customer cannot "always be right" because Noodler is always right. Time spent arguing and not promoting the company is not only unproductive but can start costing your company accounts.

Try to keep Noodler away from creative environments as well. The people who sit in beanbags and wait for inspirational ideas to pop into their heads will not jive with Noodler, who openly scoffs at emotion- or gut-based decisions. His condescending jabs will land him on the outside of the breakroom looking in.

Training/Coaching/Monitoring

If you're not much like Noodler, you might want to think about out-sourcing his training. If your company has a good self-paced study course, Noodler will eat it for breakfast. Think of Noodler as that annoying know-it-all student who sits front and center and raises his hand to answer every question, and then expands on your question and asks you a harder one to show you how smart he is. This is what you're getting into when you train Noodler. He will use the opportunity to show you what he already knows and question what you know and why he got stuck with you training him. Your biggest challenge will be re-fraining from wrapping your hands around his scrawny little neck and choking him to death.

On the monitoring front, you are tasked with holding Noodler to deadlines and, where it's warranted, brevity. This is not easy, but you need to toe the line here, or Noodler will make you absolutely nutty. Set firm deadlines and specifications, clearly state the consequences for Noodler's failing to meet them, and follow through on the consequences the minute he falters...or Noodler will eat you up.

> *Think of Noodler as that annoying know-it-all student who sits front and center and raises his hand to answer every question, and then expands on your question and asks you a harder one to show you how smart he is.*

STRATEGIES FOR MANAGING NOODLER

1	Restrict the number of items that land on Noodler's plate. He gets easily overwhelmed, and it will create nightmarish bottlenecks.
2	Work to smooth out Noodler's rough edges. Depending on his audience, he might need to deliver his facts more sensitively.
3	Set firm deadlines and strict word limits. Noodler won't meet them, so you need to build in cushion.
4	Don't waste your time micromanaging Noodler. He will be productive and hard working. Your only concern will be his focus on enough of the right things.

Handling Miscues

Noodler rarely messes up. But when he does, your initial impulse will be to call an all-hands meeting and publicly humiliate him. Please resist this impulse. Noodler will beat himself up every time he makes a mistake, and since he is likely to wallow in his own misery, that will cost you some productivity. However, if there is any doubt as to the existence of fault or who's to blame, expect Noodler to savagely defend his position and point fingers at all the other nincompoops in your team—including you.

As with all your dealings with Noodler, think through a clear strategy before you engage, head off his rebuttals, and give him a path to come out of the whole encounter in one piece.

WHAT YOU MIGHT DISCUSS WITH NOODLER

You: Noodler, what updates do you have for me? I need this to be quick.

Noodler: Hold on, Boss, let me just pull up my notes file.

You: No, no. No notes. Just give me the headlines, the bullet points.

Noodler: Oh, I see. So you don't really want the answer. I get it. You want a few sound bites that you can trot up to the big boys and make yourself look good.

You: Um, no. I have a meeting in five minutes, and I need your input, so I have something to say when they ask me what you do all day.

Noodler: I see. No, I really do. I get it. Look, why don't I go up there with you. No offense, Boss, but I'd like to let them know what I do all day, because I don't think you have enough insight into what's going on. And frankly, I'd rather sell it myself.

You: Noodler, listen to me, and listen to me good...

Noodler: Um, that's "well," Boss. You want me to listen to you well.

You: NOODLER! Tell me if I'm saying this "well": I'm going up there without you. You know why? Because I am your boss! You can tell me your updates now in bullet points, or I will go without them, and when they ask I will tell them that as far as I can tell you are unprepared, have no projections, and we might need to consider corrective action.

Character Combinations with Noodler Worth Watching

- **DOER.** Noodler will call out Doer in uncomfortable ways. He'll ask why she looks so busy. Doer will respond with her standard list of bullshit meetings and conference calls. Noodler will ask what she actually does at those meetings and on those calls. Doer will stammer unintelligibly, and you can guess where this goes. It ends with Doer in tears at her desk, wailing, "Nobody appreciates all I do!"

- **PLAYER.** Player's game will not fly by Noodler either. Player will announce his big plans to shatter the company performance record, and Noodler will put forth a treatise detailing why it can't be done. Player will try to bear hug his way out of the uncomfortable exchange, but Noodler will have nothing of it.

- **LEGEND.** Noodler's problem with Legend is that he won't give Legend the respect he deserves. In questioning Legend, Noodler will be barking up the wrong tree. Legend made his mark on the company already. He's the king. Noodler thinks too narrowly to ever become a Legend himself, but will do his best (which won't be good enough) to put a chink in Legend's armor.

Keep or Throw Back?

Look, Noodler can be a nightmare, but there is some security in having someone willing and able to comb through details that no one else wants any part of. If he terrorizes you and the setting is not a good fit, then throw him back. Otherwise, keep him around… just use him good … err, *well.*

Character Profile #8

The Doer

How Do You Know a Doer When You See One?

Man, look at her go...sprinting down hallways, eating on the fly, shouting in short bursts to you over her shoulder, scheduling back-to-back meetings all day, every day, struggling (strategically) to have her shirttails tucked in. She's the first one there in the morning, and the last one to leave. Nothing but work, work, work.

You have a volcano in your office, and her name is Doer—a loud, noisy, one-person eruption of frantic activity.

Doer leads with her busy-ness, but when it's all said and done, her bursts of energy result in complete and utter ineffectiveness.

Her nonstop activity, it turns out, is anxiety-driven, and taking on projects, however mind-numbing and insignificant, is her attempt to secure her sense of self-importance and demonstrate to herself and others that's she's needed. Keeping up the appearance of being in high demand might be the only way for her to keep her job.

The problem is that her time is cluttered with completely useless shit. When she "has a call" it's a voluntary, listen-only conference call about the company's latest HR updates. Her "presentations" are tours she leads for groups of middle school kids. Sure she's chairing a cross-functional "project," but it's really a group of environmentally conscious employees looking for ways to improve the company's recycling program.

Doer has looked like an over-extended "star" her whole life. In high school, for example, she lettered in four "varsity sports"—the Four *B*s: bowling, badminton, backgammon, and bridge—sat on the yearbook committee, decorated floats for homecoming, helped out at a preschool, volunteered in a local soup kitchen, and prepared the principal's morning announcement during homeroom. Those things were all on her college application, boldly, and proudly.

Her nonstop activity, it turns out, is anxiety-driven, and taking on projects, however mind-numbing and insignificant, is her attempt to secure her sense of self-importance and demonstrate to herself and others that's she's needed… to Doer, it's all about perceived achievement, regardless of the actual accomplishments.

What was not on her college app was that the Four *B*s took all comers, the bulk of the yearbook was completed by the control-freak art teacher, the floats were purchased pre-decorated, the preschool was owned by her mother, and all she did there was sit on the swings and talk to her boyfriend, no doubt complaining of all she had to do… you get the idea. Doer doesn't do meaningful shit… she just acts like she does. To Doer, it's all about perceived achievement, regardless of the actual accomplishments.

The deeper you dig into Doer's tangible, quantifiable production, the more obviously superficial her output.

THE DOERS

WHY YOU LOVE 'EM

- They're willing to take on anything.

- They're willing to get in early and stay late. They're always around for early or late deliveries.

- They're doers.

WHY YOU HATE 'EM

- They won't complete most of what they take on.

- What they do between their arrival and departure is equivalent to a half-day of output.

- They don't really do anything.

Real-life/Screen Examples

- **Ed Rooney**—Ferris Bueller's high school principal—not too busy to try to trap a high school kid.
- **Congress**—stirs up a whole lotta legislative dust and has little to show for it.
- **Donald Trump**—has his mitts all over everything... supermodels and all.
- **The New York Mets**—they just seem to make moves to make moves...and never really get anywhere.

A DANDY OF A DOER: ED ROONEY, THE PRINCIPAL FROM *FERRIS BUELLER'S DAY OFF*

Ed Rooney is a small-minded, paranoid, sorry excuse for an educator. He spends half his time combing through attendance records and chasing high school kids looking to take advantage of a beautiful Chicago spring day. Mr. Rooney works his ass off while never really accomplishing anything. He gets his nose bloodied by Ferris's angry, karate-kicking sister and his foot nearly torn off by a protective dog. All told, he expends a great deal of energy, all the while failing in his efforts to not come across like a complete putz.

Like Doers everywhere, Rooney does not lack for effort—he lacks for appropriate focus. If the key to catching Ferris Bueller could be found in the cure for cancer, Rooney would spend his hours hovered over a microscope. If he could only focus, Mr. Rooney could be unlocking young minds and overhauling the education system in suburban Chicago, but instead he wastes away hours unsuccessfully tracking teens on Chicago's North Side.

Ideal Settings

For at least two reasons, Doer will find success in situations in which someone is actually feeding her tasks. First, the taskmaster will be able to assign Doer meaningful, value-adding work assignments.

Second, this taskmaster will always have a sense of Doer's capacity and protect against her tendency toward overextension through volunteering. See, it's not that Doer can't be or doesn't strive to be productive—it's that she has a compulsion toward filling her time, and often does it with the first things that come her way, which are often things that don't add value. A good taskmaster will seize on Doer's energy and screen out the bullshit.

Good environments for Doer are those that carefully monitor time use and value hard, long hours. She loves bitching about how she works eighty hours a week. Accounting firms and law firms are excellent examples. Other desirable environments are those in which productivity can be objectively measured and such measures are made publicly available, like line production or call center jobs. There's nothing worse for Doer than being publicly identified as one who has wasted time on the company's dime.

One thing to watch, however, is any disconnect between the taskmaster and Doer regarding Doer's capacity. If Doer perceives that she is not being kept busy enough, then she absolutely will take on extra stuff, even outside of work, that will knock down her ability to be effective inside of work. So the taskmaster's assigned workload has to be sufficiently exhausting to prevent Doer from looking elsewhere to fill unused capacity.

Disastrous Settings

Remember, Doer takes work on a first-come, first-served basis. So environments that are structured as "free market" project-driven workplaces, such as marketing or research and development jobs in large corporations, can be especially problematic. She'll accept the first ten projects she hears about and see almost none of them through to completion. Also, Doer tends to use her self-imposed busy-ness as a cover for poor output or missed deadlines. You'll hear her say, "Sorry, I'm completely swamped" ten times a day. If no one really knows what she's doing (and if you work in one of those big, puffy corporate departments, you completely understand how that can happen), she can succeed in being completely unaccountable to anyone. Doer can also succeed in getting others to do her bidding (look out, Steady Eddie!) on the basis that she just doesn't have the time to get it all done and clearly the rest of you have not enough to do.

There is no safer way for Doer to appear off-the-charts busy than to be able to pack her calendar with completely useless management meetings, conference calls, interdepartmental meetings, and one-on-ones.

Finally, the wrong environments will promote Doer to manage others. There is no safer way for Doer to appear off-the-charts busy than to be able to pack her calendar with completely useless management meetings, conference calls, interdepartmental meetings, and one-on-ones.

Training/Coaching/Monitoring

Like anyone else, Doer must be trained and coached, but please watch for Doer to use training and coaching as a bottomless bucket. Doer will take advantage of every new training available to her and will comfortably block out her calendar and mark herself unavailable for anything else during those times. Your real chance at getting something substantial from Doer is carefully monitoring her time allocation. Though they can be perceived as being childish, activity charts and regular phone check-ins with you can be very effective in maximizing Doer's productivity.

STRATEGIES FOR MANAGING DOER

1	Schedule daily (or more frequent) activity updates so you know exactly how Doer is spending her time.
2	Make yourself or assign someone to the role of Doer's taskmaster to make sure she's taking on productive tasks.
3	Don't let Doer shoo you away with her busy-ness. She tends to use it as a shield against confessing her lack of productivity.
4	Develop a point-driven activity model to force Doer to reveal how she's spending her time.

Handling Miscues

Doer's most glaring miscues will come from missed deadlines and poor prioritization. The consequences to you and the company can be severe, so you'll need to handle these swiftly, directly, and aggressively. Keep in mind that Doer's image and anxiety are what drive her compulsive behavior, so you'll want to leverage that. Making her missed deadline public, for example, might be as eye-opening as any consequence you can dole out, provided, of course, that you can survive the blame for not monitoring it more carefully yourself.

WHAT YOU MIGHT DISCUSS WITH DOER

YOU: Doer, do you have a minute to speak with me today? I just got a call from Ross in sales, who says he needs that research right away.

DOER (sprinting down the hall): Boss, I'm totally swamped today...back-to-back calls and meetings all day.

YOU: Wait. Stop. Come back here and let's talk.

DOER: But Boss, I'm already late!

YOU: Late for what?

DOER: For a parking lot restriping committee meeting in conference room A.

YOU: Got it. I think it can wait. Doer, I need you to squeeze in Ross's sales research. That has to get done before anything else does. I think I can make a case for that outranking the parking lot meeting.

DOER: Okay, Boss, but then I have a call right after that.

YOU: For what?

DOER: The monthly management conference call.

YOU: Wait...monthly management call? I'm on that call. Why the hell are you on that call? You're not even a manager.

Doer: You must've forgotten, Boss. The CEO encouraged everyone to sit in on management calls in his initiative toward transparency and communication.

You (rubbing your temples): So your attendance is completely voluntary? Doer, get Ross his numbers before lunch. Then cancel everything else you have and come straight to my office with your calendar so we can see how you're spending your days.

Character Combinations with Doer Worth Watching

- **NOODLER.** Noodler has an eye for detail and knows a bullshitter when he sees one. Noodler knows exactly what Doer does and does not do, and how the smoke and sparks coming out of her office are merely there to hide the lack of fire. If you really need more production out of Doer, pair her with Noodler, and he will see to it that all of the tasks assigned to her are done. But be warned: if Doer is exposed by Noodler on a regular basis as an overrated asset, she will quickly begin looking elsewhere.

- **STEADY EDDIE.** Eddie is able to accomplish all Doer is unable to accomplish, without all the fanfare and excitement. Eddie can quickly fall into the trap of being Doer's lackey, and unless you watch closely, Doer will get all the credit and pass off any blame onto Eddie.

- **BADASS.** The difference between Badass and Doer is Badass takes on as heavy a workload as Doer does, but he achieves at a mind-blowing rate. Excuses and blame are not his forte, so if comparisons between Doer and Badass are being made, watch for Badass to publicly call out Doer as a bullshit artist. This one is more fire and gas than oil and water, as Doer sees herself as part Badass, and Badass loves to point out the differences.

Keep or Throw Back?

If you can bottle Doer's energy and fill her time with productive tasks, then hang on and enjoy the ride. If not, take a close look at whether you could look elsewhere for someone who could work just as hard and give you twice the output.

Character Profile #9

The Whistler

How Do You Know a Whistler When You See One?

Whistler is easy to recognize. As soon as something goes wrong, there he is at your desk, briefing you on what happened, how it happened, and most important to him, who made it happen and what Whistler thinks should be done to this person as a consequence for this misbehavior.

No one really likes Whistler, but he doesn't care—he's used to it. As a school kid, he was the self-appointed recess monitor who ratted you out when you and your classmates were playing spin the bottle behind the bushes while the teachers were gossiping, and the one who told the principal the teachers were gossiping instead of looking out for the welfare of their students.

In high school, Whistler cost your football team a playoff spot because he handed the coach photo evidence of the star quarterback drinking at a house party the weekend before. In college, Whistler was the resident assistant who wrote you up for blasting your stereo during a blowout room party. When he's not ratting out his peers, he's got his nose in the company handbook or is throwing hypotheticals by your HR rep.

Think of Whistler as your own little team police unit and policy handbook expert all wrapped up in one—which isn't necessarily a bad thing if you direct his snitching tendencies to your benefit.

Whistler spends so much time policing and busting people, he doesn't often contribute that much to your team. In fact, he can really bring down morale and instill fear that big brother (you) has enlisted a little brother (him) to watch.

THE WHISTLERS

WHY YOU LOVE 'EM

- They know all the company's policies by heart so you don't need to spend much time worrying about them.

- They monitor misbehavior by being in places you cannot.

- They will tell you everything they know about others' rules violations.

WHY YOU HATE 'EM

- They use policies maliciously to take down their peers.

- They can spend too much time monitoring and not enough time being productive.

- They think nothing of reporting *your* misdeeds to *your* boss or HR rep... so mind your Ps and Qs.

Real-life/Screen Examples

- **Chris Hansen**—the *Dateline* reporter who sets up the pedophiles. (Is it us or is he smirking when he's interviewing the scumbags he busts?)

- **Sammy "The Bull" Gravano**—a rat is a rat.

- **Woodward and Bernstein**—See? Sometimes Whistler actually does some good.

WATCH HIM WHISTLE: CHRIS HANSEN

The looks on their creepy faces are priceless. These scumbags strut into the house half-naked, with a teddy bear in one hand and a bottle of booze in the other. Hot, horny, and anxious to get it on with some minor they've been illegally soliciting online. Just when these perps think she's going to pop out of her bedroom naked and into the their arms, Chris Hansen from MSNBC's *Dateline: To Catch a Predator* cold showers them while exposing them on national freaking television.

Like any good Whistler, Hansen appears giddy as he asks these twisted perverts personal, probing questions about their sexual habits and intentions with the little ones they were hoping to meet. And not only does Hansen publicly expose them for the pedophiles they are, he publicly shares the very perverse words they used to lure their targets. As if this all weren't enough, Hansen tells them they're "free to leave," and sends them outside only

(*CONTINUED ON FOLLOWING PAGE*)

(CONTINUED)

to be given the Rodney King treatment before they are arrested by police, after which they will invariably spend time in prison running from inmate perps who invariably watched their *Dateline* episode and want to make an example of them.

Hansen's most devout followers are fellow Whistlers around the globe, who nod and smile approvingly every time they see Hansen nail another evildoer for all the world to see.

Ideal Settings

Nothing makes Whistler happier or plays more to his strength than a covert mission in which his boss enlists him. Wherever you see inefficiency and suspect foul play, get Whistler in there as discreetly and deeply as possible, and all of the mysteries in your workplace will begin making sense.

Who is playing games with their expense report? Are Badass and Butterfly really having an affair? At lunch? In the breakroom? Did Mr. Inappropriate really film it?

The only way you tolerate Whistler is if you use him. If not for people like Whistler, the Feds would still doubt the existence of the Mob.

So, even if it makes you sick to your stomach, the tabs Whistler provides you about others on your team coats that upset stomach and gives you a warm, all-knowing feeling inside. And as much as you hated Whistler when you were peers (especially if you were a Badass or Mr. Inappropriate), you will love him as his manager.

However, to keep Whistler from snooping 24/7 and actually get some work out of him, it is best to have him in a situation where employees are more or less responsible for their own time and productivity, and their numbers speak for themselves. This might force Whistler to direct more focus on his own behavior rather than that of others.

Disastrous Settings

Close-quartered, easily monitored environments like call centers or laboratories significantly decrease Whistler's importance to you, which increases the number of times you ask yourself what value this pain in the ass is adding to you and your team. In addition, the closer your people are situated in the workplace, the more obviously ostracized Whistler will be.

Just like a Mob informant who has been sniffed out as a snitch and rendered himself useless to the Feds, Whistler might work himself into perilous situations. Once the others lose trust in him you can no longer take much of the information that flows through him at face value. He will have lost the respect of his coworkers and therefore his value to you—they won't be telling him any more secrets, after all. Transfer him to another group or area of responsibility as soon as possible.

It is also important to remember that Whistler is, above all, a company man. He will sell you down the river as quickly as he sells his coworkers. So it is important to keep Whistler out of situations where he has knowledge of your questionable actions. If you've been out helping Badass fight a misdemeanor in court, or Franchise needs an extra day off for something personal, keep it to yourself.

Counterintelligence is the key here and it all becomes very "Sun Tzu." You want to keep your friends close and Whistler even closer to see every move he makes.

Training/Coaching/Mentoring

Your biggest challenge with Whistler will be keeping him from getting beat up by his peers. Yes, he needs your help to become a better team player and less of a snitch...even if it costs you valuable inside information. Help Whistler understand the personal costs of his whistle-blowing behavior, and it might make sense in select situations to have a peer or two give Whistler direct feedback about how his ratting them out makes them feel. Look, you're not here to save the world or anything, but this would be a good service to Whistler and your team. You want your people to learn how to police themselves, not avoid getting caught by you or some vigilante team member.

STRATEGIES FOR MANAGING WHISTLER

1. Set clear parameters for Whistler's snitching to you. You don't want him ratting people out in every setting, for fear that the others will know that you actually listen to what he tells you.

2. Keep Whistler focused on his own behavior, and specifically watch for signs that he is using his whistle-blowing to push attention away from himself.

3. Since you're stuck with him, you might as well use him. Signal to Whistler the information you're most interested in getting, and he will sniff it out.

4	Schedule periodic time with the Human Resources rep, not only so you can warn Human Resources about Whistler's tendencies, but also so you can monitor what Whistler is feeding her.
5	Be sure to verify Whistler's story before acting too severely. Think *New York Times* editorial requirements versus those of TMZ.
6	In one-on-ones with Whistler, get him to focus on his own behavior rather than that of others (soak him for the info about others in more clandestine visits outside the context of management). You might find that Whistler is ratting people out to take the focus off his own less-than-stellar contributions.
7	Find out about his ideal career trajectory…let him know what he needs to do to achieve it. He will.

Handling Miscues

When Whistler screws up, his peers will want him publicly tarred and feathered. You know where they're coming from—this is a very good day for them, and there's a part of you too that wants to see Whistler get his. But you need to take the high road here and protect Whistler from abuse that is disproportionate to the crime he committed. Give Whistler the same consequences you would anyone else.

WHAT YOU MIGHT DISCUSS WITH WHISTLER

YOU: Whistler, how are you today? Have a seat.

WHISTLER: Hey, Boss. I was just speaking to Needy Ned. He was about to explain to me how he got blamed for that last mis-shipment, but it was really Butterfly who entered the data incorrectly, and Steady Eddie was standing right there watching. Are you going to say something to Butterfly?

YOU: Probably not. That was a small mistake. The customer understood and actually kept the merchandise. It's no big deal.

WHISTLER: But Boss, what about that time the same thing happened with Future and you reamed him? Shouldn't things be the same for everyone? Do you think HR would think that's right?

YOU: I'd be happy to discuss with HR if Future—not you—brought it to their attention. The truth is, how I responded to Future was appropriate to that situation with Future. In this situation, Butterfly's mistake—or whoever's mistake it was—did not rise to the same level....

YOU (whispering): So, I heard Franchise got a job offer from that new company on the East Side. Is that true?

WHISTLER: Whoa, that is news to me, Boss. I am on it! I will make it my business to know before lunch!

Character Combinations with Whistler Worth Watching

- **BADASS.** Talk about fire and gasoline. Badass is Whistler's wet dream. He calls Badass a rebel, a menace, a disgrace to the good name of the company. Badass simply refers to him as "The Rat Bastard." The only time to combine these two is if and when you are at wit's end with Badass and his production has begun to shrink in comparison to his irreverence. You might want to alert the local police, however, for Badass might just unload his pistol on Whistler.

- **FUTURE.** Whistler may actually keep Future on his toes and away from any temptations he may have to mature into Slacker. To Whistler, there is only one way to do things: the right way. Any temptations Future has to stray will be doused if he knows Whistler is waiting in the wings. Be careful, however, not to positively reinforce Whistler's behavior, for you wouldn't want Future to assume that role. You've got plans for Future, and they involve others actually liking him.

- **MR. INAPPROPRIATE.** Just for your own amusement.

Keep or Throw Back?

Unfortunately, once somebody is identified as a Whistler there are very few places they can go. None of his peers trust him. You don't trust him. And those above you will soon tire of his act. Use him for what you need him for and then find the next one after his peers force him to leave.

Character Profile #10

ADHD Butterfly

Starting Five

Utility Players

Benchwarmers

Trading Block Candidates

How Do You Know an ADHD Butterfly When You See One?

The things that make ADHD Butterfly a good employee are the same things that make her a nightmare to manage and work with. Yes, she is gregarious, friendly, engaging, and has heard her whole life, "You are such a people person." But ADHD Butterfly flits unpredictably from activity to activity, without worry or any real understanding of priority. She mingles in other departments, often for hours on end, while she completely neglects her own responsibilities.

As a result, Butterfly can go many consecutive days without accomplishing much of anything. Much to your consternation, Butterfly focuses her attention on all the wrong details. For example, she knows everyone's name in the mailroom but can't remember those of her customers.

Most people don't like ADHD Butterfly. She's the one in the office who talks loudly and incessantly, and is blissfully ignorant of the fact that while she is talking, everyone is rolling their eyes at each other in complete disgust. If only she would shut the hell up every once in awhile, others might be able to get some work done.

Butterfly has a perverse, insatiable thirst for gossip. And though she can often be heard at the water cooler shrieking in horror upon hearing about a colleague's misfortune, she appears undeniably satisfied by receiving the bad news. It wouldn't be fair to say that Butterfly doesn't care about others, it's just that she doesn't really care whether the others are good, bad, or indifferent, as long as they just give her some interesting dirt.

The point most obviously missed by Ms. Butterfly is that workers need to work. The Butterfly fails to understand that a job merely begins with the social bonds and relationships and is never a substitute for production.

What makes Butterfly potentially valuable is her undying energy, which, when corralled, can be used to get some stuff done. And, as long as the work you dole out to her is varied and interesting enough to keep her engaged, Butterfly can deliver. Think how productive your bipolar friends are when they're in their manic phase—ADHD Butterfly can paint fifteen walls until three in the morning, too!

> *Butterfly has a perverse, insatiable thirst for gossip. And though she can often be heard at the water cooler shrieking in horror upon hearing about a colleague's misfortune, she appears undeniably satisfied by receiving the bad news.*

ADHD BUTTERFLIES

WHY YOU LOVE 'EM

- They have boundless energy.

- They love the company of others.

- They know everyone in the office.

WHY YOU HATE 'EM

- Their energy knows no bounds.

- Nobody really likes their company...particularly when they're working.

- They visit everyone in the office every day, sometimes more than once a day.

Real-life/Screen Examples

- **Robin Williams**—ever see him as a late-night talk show guest? Right, so have we.
- **Kelly from *The Office***—train wreck.
- **MTV on-air "talent"**—veejays used to be so cool.
- **The Cameraman from *The Blair Witch Project***—we still have headaches.

BIG SCREEN BUTTERFLY: ROBIN WILLIAMS

Ever see Robin Williams on the *Tonight Show with Jay Leno*? He scoots around the stage like a water bug, jumps tangentially from topic to topic, sweats profusely, and completely dominates the conversation. It's uncomfortable.

You love his energy, and you think he's sort of funny, but then he just starts to wear you out with his nonstop impressions and Tourette Syndrome–like body movements. He doesn't listen to a word Jay says (not that he'd add much value anyway), and basically spends his twenty-minute segment barking at the audience. You wish he would take a breath so he would just shut his mouth for a second and give the television audience a break.

Ideal Settings

Butterfly requires rigid guidelines, a laser-focused job description, and enforcers in place to crack the whip when she (inevitably) veers. But while clearly defined nine-to-five desk jobs might help rein Butterfly in, she won't likely last under such tight wraps. Butterfly needs to, well, fly. A setting with a greater likelihood of success is one that offers Butterfly freedom of movement coupled with carefully monitored activity requirements (e.g., number of clients called, number of business cards picked up, number of client satisfaction surveys received). Note that here the emphasis is on volume, which will cater to Butterfly's affinity for fluttering. Restricting what (or whom) she's fluttering to will hopefully lead to more consistent productivity.

Harnessing and controlling Butterfly's sociability is not easy, but if your expectations and requirements are stated often and clearly enough she has the potential to become a solid employee.

Disastrous Settings

If left to her own devices with little or no supervision, Butterfly can go entire weeks fluttering from water cooler to cubicles to conference rooms, sharing gossip, photos of the family, and tales from her latest vacation. Absent structure and accountability, Butterfly will haunt you with her complete lack of productivity. Setups for disaster include telecommuting arrangements, frequent out-of-office work without throughout-the-day phone check-ins, and any job that requires Butterfly to sit at a desk and focus for large blocks of time—she just ain't going to do it!

Training/Coaching/Mentoring

The biggest mistake managers can make with Butterfly is trying to pound attention span into her. She will never internalize your time management and organizational techniques. Butterfly tends to be a visual learner (please don't give her lengthy academic books to read), so she will tend to do better by watching you first and then very soon thereafter repeating the task and hearing your objective feedback. Furthermore, whenever possible, training and coaching in her presence will serve you and Butterfly well. She is, after all, a social being, so she will respond favorably to you being there. In addition, your presence will help you keep her focused on what's at hand. If you need to speak with her, do it in person instead of on the phone. Risk phone sessions at your peril, for she is likely texting her BFFs while you're disseminating your juicy management nuggets.

STRATEGIES FOR MANAGING BUTTERFLY

1   Keep Butterfly on a very short leash … give easy-to-measure requirements and ding her for every one she fails to meet. If nothing else, it will start building material for you to take to HR when you're looking to remove her.

2   Enlist Whistler to monitor Butterfly's fluttering.

3   Institute frequent e-mail or telephone check-in requirements so you know where she is and what she has been doing.

4   Wherever possible, remove distractions. For example, seat her in the windowless office off the storage room in the basement, block Internet access, and deter others from visiting with her on social matters.

5   Build in opportunities for Butterfly to stretch her wings. Binding her to a chair for hours on end will make her (and, ultimately, you) batty.

6   Capitalize on her sociability. She'll be a hit at conventions, for example. Just make sure you require her to pick up and hand out a minimum number of business cards.

Handling Miscues

Just like a puppy who refuses to heel on command, Butterfly will only respond to pure, unadulterated in-your-face criticism. Subtle hints and humor-laced messages simply do not work. "Butterfly, you must stop socializing when you should be working" will always be more effective than "Hey, Butterfly, how about working the rest of your body as much as you work your mouth?"

Where most employees read between the lines and get your implied messages, minced words are lost on Butterfly. She will just interpret them as friendly banter and construe them as "Boss didn't really mean that... he's just messing with me." It is imperative that she knows in no uncertain terms exactly what you find fault with.

WHAT YOU MIGHT DISCUSS WITH ADHD BUTTERFLY

YOU: Butterfly, how did you make out with that customer's complaint that came in? Was the merchandise really that bad?

BUTTERFLY: Oh, Rose? The lady in Omaha? Do you know she actually had a niece that went to school with a cousin of Warren Buffet's barber? Amazing.

YOU: Really?

BUTTERFLY: Yes... the same niece also married a cabdriver from New York. A Russian guy, I believe.

YOU (pause and deep breath): Um, but did you get a photo of the merchandise? Or a written complaint on their letterhead so we can send it to the vendor? You know, did you follow any of the standard procedures?

(CONTINUED ON FOLLOWING PAGE)

Benchwarmers

(CONTINUED)

BUTTERFLY: Well, Rose—that's Stella's aunt by the way....

YOU: Who the hell is Stella?

BUTTERFLY: Warren Buffet's maid, Boss. Pay attention. Well anyway, she's the one who makes the final quality-control decisions there, and she is out on vacation. They have the absolute best vacation policy. We should have that here.

YOU: Wait, so you never got the right person on the phone?

BUTTERFLY: Nope, but I sure did find a dear phone buddy in Rose.

YOU (reaching for aspirin): Get out of my office.

Character Combinations with Butterfly Worth Watching

- **STEADY EDDIE.** Eddie's stoic nature and methodical, strict adherence to policy and production may be a great influence on Butterfly. While she will never stop being the social creature she inherently is, by teaming her with someone who produces quietly behind the scenes, you may piece together a decent team. Butterfly will kick up dust and Eddie will settle it.

- **SLACKER.** This combination is a disaster waiting to happen. Slacker and Butterfly are both defined by their lack of productivity. The only difference is that

Slacker consciously seeks ways to be unproductive, while Butterfly flutters into them. Slacker can easily stir up Butterfly in a way that creates distractions that will spring Slacker from work. Watch for Slacker to manufacture a good gasp at a juicy Internet gossip headline just to dislodge Butterfly from her seat and bridge the gap between mid-afternoon and the close of business.

- **FUTURE.** Be careful here. You want Future to learn from the best and see business is business. While personality and social skills are certainly assets, there must be pragmatic, tangible substance at the end of the week if you wish to get a paycheck. Idle chatter doesn't pay the bills. If Future gets a sense that random, unproductive socializing goes unchecked, you will have sent him the wrong message and compromised your team's productivity.

Keep or Throw Back?

As long as you can successfully police Butterfly without exhausting too many resources, and find ways to channel Butterfly's social tendencies, she might be worth keeping. But if you find Butterfly's distractions adversely affecting team performance and commanding too much of your management time and energy, do yourself and your company a favor and set Butterfly free.

Character Profile #11

Needy Ned

How Do You Know a Needy Ned When You See One?

Needy Ned is the quintessential sheep who requires a shepherd to tell him where and when to move. He needs the company of others, endless reinforcement that he's doing okay, and constant reassurance that he's going to be safe.

Don't look now, but Needy Ned is at your office door right now, for the seventeenth time today, to seek your approval to run to the bathroom.

There is always one kid afraid of the dark...and of the deep end of the swimming pool...and one who runs in terror from circus clowns.* Adventure is not his strong suit, and neither is going it alone.

Ned is capable of huge success, as long as you are with him in the room and nodding approvingly.

---

* We're with Ned on the clowns. What kind of an adult would take that job anyway? The shoes? The hair? Disconcerting.

Ned knows everything he needs to know and more, but he nevertheless pounds on you and others for confirmation. You see him coming, and you want to dive into a utility closet.

Substance and knowledge, even if extracted as painfully as if it were abscessed or compounded, is often more valuable and harder to find than style. Ned has it … but how to get it out of him without holding his hand? That's the big challenge with Ned.

NEEDY NEDS

WHY YOU LOVE 'EM	WHY YOU HATE 'EM
• They will never, ever make a decision that might jeopardize you, your team, or the company without your express authorization.	• They will never, ever make a decision— no matter how insignificant—without your authorization.
• They are singularly devoted to pleasing and doing right by you and the company.	• In their never-ending interest to please, they constantly check with you to make sure that what they've done is pleasing to you.
• They know every detail in the company policy handbook.	• They constantly check the company policy handbook to confirm what they already know.

Real-life/Screen Examples

- **That clingy high school sweetheart**—the one who haunted your locker between every period—yeah, you know the one—wrapped around you like a tight wool sweater, always asking how much you love her.

- **Cameron Frye (Ferris Bueller's best friend)**—remember the debate he had with himself before finally driving over to pick up Ferris?

- **The forty-year-old virgin**—Forty years old? Seriously? He must be married.

NEEDY NADINE (NED'S FEMALE COUNTERPART): YOUR CLINGY HIGH SCHOOL SWEETHEART

She's lurking at your locker—again. Now she's glaring at you because you had a friendly conversation with a girl in your math class...about homework due that day. She bursts into tears because you didn't return her call... even though she knew you were at practice when she called you. Like any good Needy Ned, your high school sweetheart wants a monopoly on your attention, and she is willing to engage in behavior that will make you absolutely hate her to achieve it. She employs despicable tactics, like invoking guilt through racking sobs, talking to your mother about your emotional vacancy, and flirting openly with your best friend to get you jealous. You can't shake this little stalker, even when you break up with her.

(CONTINUED ON FOLLOWING PAGE)

Benchwarmers

(CONTINUED)

You spend most of your time with her wondering why you ever thought this would work, because she was needy from the moment you met. Maybe it felt good to be needed at first... now it just feels like being draped in an Irish knit straightjacket on a sweltering July afternoon.

Ideal Settings

Ned thrives in settings in which chains of command and organizational hierarchy are rigidly adhered to, and excessive worry about detail, getting the green light from up the chain, and getting everything absolutely perfect the very first time are paramount. NASA and the Bush-Cheney administration are examples of organizations packed with Needy Neds, as both settings call for the little guys on the ground to do their research, reach a conclusion, and then check with the guy next up on the totem pole to see what they should do about it. Nobody move an inch until we say so! Workplaces laced with this sort of institutionally driven paranoia are Needy Ned's sweet spot. Not only will he *not* get lambasted for his endless checking, he'll be praised for it. Government agencies, law firms, and the military tend to be favorable environments for Ned. He lives for red tape.

Disastrous Settings

Ned will crash and burn in any environment that requires independent thinking, action, or decision making. Ned lacks confidence in his own ability, so he will constantly second-guess his impulses, and turn to you for affirmation. Assuming you work in an environment in which you require Ned to be his own man and make his own decisions, Ned is bound to drive you nutty. Outside sales environments, fast-paced start-ups, and creative environments and thinly staffed work environments will cause Ned (and you) pain.

Training/Coaching/Monitoring

Ned has been needy since childhood. No classes, therapy, or Dale Carnegie books are going to change that. He is a paranoid little wimp. If he's been doing his job for a reasonably long time, and still finds himself paralyzed without constant reassurance, then forget about training and coaching. You'll actually be feeding the beast more of what he wants but doesn't need. He'll internalize that his incapacity leads to more training and coaching, which makes him happy, so he'll act increasingly incapacitated to get more training and coaching. See this vicious cycle? Yes, it's ugly.

The interesting management diagnosis of Ned occurs in your first few months with him on your team. Many new hires will be appropriately cautious about making decisions without the go-ahead from above—this is healthy. During that initial stage, people who aren't Ned can look an awful lot like him. Your challenge is making sure that you deliver these newbies all the training, coaching, and mentoring they need to act independently before making the determination that you're actually dealing with a Needy Ned. So when a new hire with Ned-like qualities is driving you crazy with his neediness (or you find yourself with more than one Ned), you might first take a look at what training and monitoring you have in place. Maybe they're not getting enough from you. Maybe you're second-guessing their decisions and encouraging them to be needier than they normally would be. It's worth a look in the mirror...we're just saying.

STRATEGIES FOR MANAGING NEEDY NED

1   Make sure he has everything he needs from a training perspective at his fingertips. If he doesn't know what he needs to know, that's on you, not Ned.

2   Praise Ned every single time he makes an independent decision. Think of Ned like a nervous little lab rat who needs a flavor-packed pellet every time he makes a move in the right direction. This can get tiresome and cause others to roll their eyes in disgust, but it has the chance of saving you time and energy in the long haul.

3   Resist the urge to shock Ned into independent action. Like the parent who throws his nervous kid into the deep end in hopes that he suddenly puts his hours of swimming lessons to use and stays afloat, this strategy can have catastrophic consequences and actually cause Ned to regress, not develop.

4   When all else fails, hook Ned up with a Steady Eddie-type mentor and have him pound on Eddie for a while. Eddie is likely to be more patient than you, and it will free you up to spend your time more productively.

Handling Miscues

Because he's constantly checking for your thumbs-up before he acts, Ned will not tend to make many mistakes (sometimes you'd actually kill for him to make more, which would give you evidence of risk-taking—a trait foreign to Ned). But Ned will make occasional mistakes that require your attention. How you handle these are absolutely critical to Ned's development. If he sees the world doesn't end when he makes a mistake, then he just might be more confident making a move without you the next time.

Look, Ned is a Ned, so your reaction might not make a difference at all—he might perceive it to be too strong no matter how sensitively delivered. But rest assured, if you blast Ned for a mistake he makes, he will never, ever make an independent decision again.

WHAT YOU MIGHT DISCUSS WITH NEEDY NED

YOU: How is that presentation coming along for next week's board meeting?

NED: I actually found a way to get a better price than what you and I originally hammered out. It will mean more profits for the company. I also found a better shipping method that will save our client money.

YOU: Great. I look forward to seeing it and hearing your spin on it in the presentation.

NED: What? Wait. You're going to review and comment on it, right? And I can't present to the board. Are you effing kidding me?

(CONTINUED ON FOLLOWING PAGE)

(CONTINUED)

You: Dude. Chill. You know this stuff. Every nook and cranny of it. I've reviewed your last five presentations, and I've never recommended substantive changes. Granted, the last few times I've presented the material, but then I ended up deferring to you on almost all questions because I didn't know the material well enough. Ned...every single time we...look, Ned... you are...(sigh)...just do it, Ned. Please.

Character Combinations with Needy Ned Worth Watching

- **NOODLER.** Noodler and Ned share attention to detail. The major difference is that Ned is tending to details out of fear of screwing up, while Noodler is tending to details to throw his well-conceived conclusions in the face of those who think they know better. Ned is more obsessed with pleasing others than Noodler, who couldn't care less about pleasing anyone other than the gods of reason.

- **STEADY EDDIE.** Eddie might be the one who can save Ned's job (and your sanity). Ned and Eddie are a match made in heaven. Eddie's patience, tendency toward accommodation, and drive for team harmony will nurture Ned in a way that gets him out of your hair. The only risk here is that Ned comes to rely too heavily on Eddie, and finds his development stunted. Ned longs for attention and nurturing, and Eddie longs to dole out healthy doses of both. Ned needs his hand held through a project? Eddie is there to hold it. Ned needs someone to help him role play with him on customer service escalation calls? Eddie puts his fake phone to his ear. Ned needs his butt wiped delicately because he's been suffering from hemorrhoids? Eddie goes running for the toilet paper.

- **BADASS.** The Badass–Ned combo is more fun for intra-office fireworks and entertainment than anything else. Ned's paralysis absent approval from above will literally drive Badass off the deep end. If you hear a loud rant coming from the conference room where Badass and Ned have been holed up trying to get a report finalized, run quickly so you can pry Badass's hands from Ned's throat.

Keep or Throw Back?

If you are needed for every indecisive moment during the course of a day, do you really need Ned at all? Ned's is a high-pressure job, right? If you can't take the heat, get your ass out of the kitchen, right?

Despite his obvious insecurities and endless drain on your most valuable resource—your time—Ned adds value because of his undying work ethic. He knows the product, the accounts, your policies, procedures, and the lay of the industry—he would be completely paralyzed by fear if he didn't. You need to find ways to keep Ned around if a neurotically detailed grunt is really vital to your team.

However, if you work in an environment that requires independent action, then Ned (assuming he's not just a newbie that hasn't been properly trained) might never cut it in your office. And, in that case, you might want to cut your losses now, or you risk arrest for frustration-driven assault and battery.

Character Profile #12

Mr. Inappropriate
(Yes, It's Almost Always 'Mister')

How Do You Know a Mr. I When You See One?

You cringe at his ethnic jokes and vulgar comments to female colleagues. You wince as he burps and farts in front of his clients. You hurriedly pretend to hear someone calling you when he moves to show you naked pictures of his girlfriend.

Meet Mr. Inappropriate. An HR nightmare. A lawsuit waiting to happen. A complete pervert... and (unfortunately) one of your consistent performers.

Mr. Inappropriate shows up to work late with his suits wrinkled, his hair in a tussle, and with traces of booze on his breath. Did he sleep in the car or in the bar?

His paperwork and losing racetrack tickets are poking out of his well-worn briefcase, and you can't send him a voicemail or e-mail because his inboxes are always full with messages from his bookie, creditors, or one of his three ex-wives.

What he lacks in polish, he certainly makes up for in spit.

Old school, "I-made-you-laugh-so-give-me-what-I-want" workplace communication techniques are a lost art. A generation of (mostly) white businessmen made an impressive living leading with off-color jokes. And because their clients, co-workers, and bosses were also mostly white and male, their jokes helped them make up for their shortcomings and kept them in the business.

But we're living in different times now, and the dirty jokes just don't fly like they once had. Have you seen Andrew Dice Clay lately on something other than *Celebrity Apprentice*? Exactly. His dirty jokes are as likely to horrify as please, and they might just land you, his boss, in hot water.

It's easy to write off Mr. Inappropriate as a politically incorrect dinosaur, obsolete in this day and age, because, well, he is. Keep in mind, however, that he has at least one very valuable lesson to offer today's managers: *if you can get your clients, co-workers, and bosses comfortable and relaxed in your presence, they will withstand almost anything as long as they see net positive results from you!*

MR. INAPPROPRIATES

WHY YOU LOVE 'EM	WHY YOU HATE 'EM
• They remind us of our favorite dirty old uncle.	• They're always a threat to get us in trouble.
• They actually enjoy interacting with clients… even the difficult ones.	• They're unkempt and smelly.
• Every team needs a mascot.	• We've heard all their jokes a million times before.

Real-Life/Screen Examples

- **Howard Stern**—this guy's whole game is shock and awe.

- **Rodney Dangerfield in** *Caddyshack*—"What, when you buy a hat like this I bet you get a free bowl of soup, huh? Oh, it looks good on you though."

- **John Belushi in** *Animal House*—the human zit impression still ranks on all-time lists of egregiously inappropriate behavior.

- **Booger from** *Revenge of the Nerds*—oh yes, he picked 'em and ate 'em.

- **Roseanne Barr**—this Ms. Inappropriate intentionally shanked the National Anthem.

- **Charles Barkley**—this might not be fair to Sir Charles, but he certainly pressed the limits of the NBA's tolerance.

MR. INAPPROPRIATE ON THE AIRWAVES: HOWARD STERN

He's all about shock value via T&A jokes—that's his whole game. He's not really as funny as he is appalling, and now that he's on satellite radio he seems tickled by his license to drop F-bombs every five minutes.

But despite it all, Howard Stern still commands a devoted fan base of other Mr. Is (enough of one, at least, to magically keep satellite radio afloat). Stern constantly seeks to outdo himself: he began by interviewing strippers on the air and asking about their boobs, then graduated to

(*CONTINUED ON FOLLOWING PAGE*)

Benchwarmers

(CONTINUED)

having them actually strip on the air so he could see and touch their boobs, and moved on to tricks that cannot be described in a business book.

The only difference between Stern and the Mr. I on your team is that you can turn the dial to get away from Stern.

Ideal Setting

Mr. Inappropriate seems to gravitate toward flexible, out-of-office work environments. Maybe it's the relatively unpatrolled nature of the job, or the human interaction, or the constantly shifting audiences. Mr. Inappropriate thrives in old, industrial, male-dominated industries in which Mr. I's shtick still tends to be well-received. Old, friendly, blue-collar corporate types who can "take a joke" (no matter how out of place in any other context) will always give Mr. Inappropriate more face time than they will to a politically correct, fresh-faced kid in a pinstripe suit. They just "connect" with them.

Mr. Inappropriate hates to be scolded—especially publicly— for his outdated humor (it shines a bright light on how obsolete he's becoming), so strategic and relatively discreet policing of his behavior will keep him in check. Managers who can find a way to channel Mr. Inappropriate's charm and good humor, while stripping away the harassment lawsuit stuff (or at least keeping it in the shadows and dark alleys) will be the real winners...because in the right environment, this guy will produce results.

Disastrous Settings

Try to keep Mr. Inappropriate away from church groups, ladies' teas, and all settings steeped in political correctness. Corporate cultures that call for polished presentation and team selling will kick him to the curb. Also, environments that don't have built in policing mechanisms could result in a rash of HR reports. Left unchecked, Mr. Inappropriate will fail to see his behavior as, well, inappropriate, and he will jeopardize not only his reputation but that of your company's.

> *Try to keep Mr. Inappropriate away from church groups, ladies' teas, and all settings steeped in political correctness.*

Mr. I works without a net, and those unfamiliar with him, his brand of humor, or personality type will raise hell when he rubs them the wrong way. No matter how well he performs, if he takes down your name or that of your employer, you will regret even ever knowing Mr. Inappropriate. Tread cautiously.

Training/Coaching/Monitoring

While Mr. Inappropriate seems unwilling to clean up his act, it might be more helpful to view him as unaware of what qualifies as truly offensive in corporate America today. Some call him a pig, others groan audibly, and others still just walk away. But this is his entire act, and he's been getting those reactions for a very long time. This man needs someone in a position of authority (namely you, his boss) to observe his social disgraces, give him plain feedback about their effect on business, and brainstorm with him to develop different ways of tapping his ability to charm and connect while toning down his offensiveness. In order to do this, you need to observe him interacting with others firsthand.

STRATEGIES FOR MANAGING MR. INAPPROPRIATE

1	Don't laugh at Mr. Inappropriate's inappropriate jokes, even if they're funny as hell. It really does reinforce the very behavior you're trying to see less of.
2	Steer him to appropriate tasks and interactions with those in a handful of appropriate industries…those more likely to embrace his dirty-old-man persona.
3	Show him that you're firm, be clear what you'll tolerate and what you won't, and confront him immediately and assertively when he breaks the rules.
4	Reward his results, not the faulty parts of the process.
5	When you're delivering the tough feedback, keep your focus solely on the bad behavior and don't make it a personal attack on Mr. I.

Handling Miscues

Where Mr. Inappropriate is concerned, you need to follow up on complaints from clients and colleagues immediately, directly, and with a pen and paper in hand so you have the story ready when HR comes a-knocking. At some point, if the behavior does not diminish, you will be forced to start drawing firm, bold lines. If Mr. I crosses these lines, *you* will initiate HR action. Look, you might not be the most sensitive cat in the world, but you're no Mr. Inappropriate, and you're sure as hell not going to lose your job over him.

WHAT YOU MIGHT DISCUSS WITH MR. INAPPROPRIATE

You: Mr. I, can I give you some feedback?

Mr. I: Sure, kid.

You: I heard you tell Al that "hung like a bear" joke.

Mr. I: Love that joke…did I ever tell the time I told that joke to a client in the middle of an escalated service call and I saved the sales order for two hundred black-and-white television sets?

You: No…but I'm wondering what Al's daughter thought of it…she was standing there when you told it, and I got the sense from the grimace on her face that she didn't like it as much as you and the old man did.

Mr. I: Look, I've been doing business with the old man for twenty-two years…the guy loves a good joke.

You: I get it…I'm just wondering if you've got a few that might resonate with mixed audiences. I'm pretty sure most women find jokes like that offensive…HR's already called you in, and further reprimands could start having a major impact on your employment here.

Mr. I: Well, there's that one about the talking Chihua-hua and the leopard…

You: That sounds better…tell you what, when things get sticky on the next service call you're on, why don't you lead with that one and let's see how it goes over.

Mr. I: You got it, kid. Let's see how it goes.

Character Combinations with Mr. I Worth Watching

- **THE BADASS.** Badass is not offended by Mr. I (she's not really offended by anyone), she just doesn't have time for his shit all the time. Why tell a stupid joke when you could just cut to the chase, find out if those around you can help you, and, if not, move on? Mr. I doesn't have to worry about Badass reporting him to HR, but he will feel her wrath if his act somehow manages to get in the way of her success. Badass is about results and Mr. I is about, well, being Mr. I. His shtick wears thin on everyone before long. The Steady Eddies and Needy Neds of the world have learned to live with it. Badass has the balls to tell him to cut the shit.

- **THE PLAYER.** In many ways, Player is everything Mr. I is not. Player goes out of his way to say things he knows the listener will want to hear and Mr. I just says whatever filthy words come to mind. But Player, ever the good soldier, will laugh heartily at Mr. I's filth. Mr. I will leave happy that he made yet another one laugh, and Player will go gossip about what a pig Mr. I is.

- **THE WHISTLER.** Mr. I is the Whistler's wildest fantasy. The company handbook is Mr. I's playground and Whistler's bible, so Mr. I gives Whistler reason to live. Whistler is no fool: She knows you want to know every wrong move Mr. I makes, so she'll be on his tail 24/7. But any attempt by Whistler to keep Mr. I in line will likely backfire. Mr. I has been battling the armies of do-gooders his whole life, so he'll make it his crusade to shock and awe Whistler with material that would offend Richard Pryor, let alone the HR department. This relationship is plainly combustible.

Keep or Throw Back?

Even if Mr. I is performing like crazy, you need to protect your reputation. The cost-benefit equation here is simple to state but admittedly more complicated to compute: when the adverse impact of Mr. Inappropriate's poor behavior outweighs the benefits of his productivity, then he must go. If you observe measurable improvement after you intervene, and you think you can sufficiently muzzle him while keeping performance up, then you can probably make the case to keep him.

Character Profile #13

The Slacker

How Do You Know a Slacker When You See One?

The first thing that jumps off Slacker's resume is where he earned his undergraduate degree. Wow, what a school. What is he doing sitting across from me trying to get a job? With a pedigree like that…hmm.

And when you speak with him, you're startled by how polished he is. He's articulate, thoughtful, and personable. But look how many jobs he's had since he graduated from that great school. Or that he never seems to have earned a promotion anywhere. Or that the jobs he's had don't seem commensurate with his Ivy League education. When you ask him about his career aspirations, you're underwhelmed. This guy should be aiming at the C-suite, and instead he's talking about "carving out a comfortable life" for himself and earning enough money so he doesn't have to stress over whether to walk the course or rent a golf cart.

You know he's smart—your good looks alone don't get you into the Ivies. Maybe he's a late bloomer. Maybe he took a few too many bong hits during his fraternity's rush parties. Something doesn't quite compute. Maybe he's never had a winning boss like you to take him under his wing and tap that fabulous potential that is lying within. "Damn," you say to yourself as you're licking your lips just looking at this hunk of meat across the desk from you, "I've got to get me some of that."

Fast forward twelve months. His grandmothers have died four times. He called in sick on opening day, and was interviewed on television—drunk—at the ballgame. The only reliable place to locate him is on the golf course on a sunny Friday afternoon (his golf reference in the interview a year ago should have tipped you off).

If he were half as driven to produce as he is to get away with not producing, this guy would be a Franchise. Instead, he's just a Slacker.

THE SLACKERS

WHY YOU LOVE 'EM

- They're packed with the three *P*s:
  - Polish
  - Pedigree
  - Potential

- They make for a great partner in your golf club's member-guest.

- They're so lucky that they sometimes fall ass-backward into a great piece of business.

WHY YOU HATE 'EM

- All you ultimately get from them is the three *D*s:
  - Disappointment
  - Difficulty in tracking down
  - Damn good excuses

- They spend more time on the proverbial golf course than they do working.

- They usually deliver results that amount to a pile of shit.

Real-life/Screen Examples

- **George W. Bush**—took more vacation days than any president in U.S. history.

- **Ferris Bueller**—legendary teenage, school-skipping slacker.

- **Billy Madison**—Adam Sandler's lovable character loafing poolside sucking off Daddy's dime.

- **Mallory Keaton (Michael J. Fox's sister on *Family Ties*)**—she might be a slacker…or she also might just be dumb.

- **Paul Allen**—Co-founder of Microsoft who cashed out early. While Bill Gates is busy trying to save the world, this guy is buying shitty sports teams, the world's biggest yachts and playing a really bad blues guitar.

SLACKING IN THE OVAL OFFICE: GEORGE W. BUSH

You could argue that George W. Bush treated his eight years in office as if they were one long victory lap through his senior year in high school. GWB took more vacation days than any sitting president, logging a healthy 487 days at Camp David and 490 at his ranch in Crawford, Texas, amounting to roughly 30 percent of his presidential (using that term loosely) tenure.

Look, we like to chill as much as the next guy, but we're thinking the leader of the free world ought to be more focused on reining in terror and preventing the collapse of

(CONTINUED ON FOLLOWING PAGE)

(CONTINUED)

the world economy than clearing brush and perfecting his golf swing (might have been nice if he at least thumbed through some books). Like any good Slacker, Bush was adept at dodging questions about his prolonged and frequent absences, and distracted us all by making sweeping claims (from his Camp David hammock) about the agenda of the left-wing media.

Ideal Settings

Slacker is all about meeting the bare minimum. He's adept at doing just enough to keep his job. Slacker views exerting even an ounce of energy more on work than he has to as energy that would have been better spent on his golf swing. So Slacker thrives (or at least sucks the least) in environments in which the threat of getting fired is real (and there aren't loads of other equivalent opportunities otherwise available), the objectives he must meet to retain his job are objective and clear, and you have sufficient policing mechanisms in place to monitor Slacker's performance relative to the standards you set.

If you have these things in place, then you can actually soak Slacker for performance. You then simply set the minimum requirements at a level that, if achieved, allows you to comfortably keep Slacker on the team.

As for specifics, look for roles in which productivity can be clearly and objectively measured, such as sales and production. Lay out the bare minimum quotas, and watch Slacker creep precisely up to them.

Disastrous Settings

Slacker is immature and possesses little self-discipline. Any sort of interdependent team environment, creative function, or oversight role, in which Slacker's individual contributions are difficult or impossible to measure, is likely to encourage his tendencies to cut corners. Others will mutter about him behind his back, complaining that they can't find him, and that he hasn't returned a call or e-mail in weeks. Your challenge in these settings is leverage. How do you quantify Slacker's contributions (or lack thereof)? What would you say to your HR rep who wants you to substantiate why you want to put Slacker on a performance management contract? It's a total nightmare for you and everyone involved, though you should invite him to your member-guest game before you have to let him go, as his golf game is certain to be in fine form.

> *Slacker is immature and possesses little self-discipline. Any sort of interdependent team environment, creative function, or oversight role, in which Slacker's individual contributions are difficult or impossible to measure, is likely to encourage his tendencies to cut corners.*

Training/Coaching/Monitoring

Your issue with Slacker is not his institutional or industry knowledge—he has the goods he needs to perform at a very high level. Your issue is your ability to measure Slacker's productivity and then to communicate clearly the gap between what he's delivering at present and what you need him to deliver. Give these discussions a lot of thought. Maybe Slacker has a required first-thing-in-the-morning and end-of-day check-in meeting with you every day. Perhaps have him shoot you an e-mail each time he's going to leave his desk, or spot-check his cubicle a few times each day and leave a Post-It Note with the time you were there and saw him missing.

You micromanage Slacker because he will not do any meaningful work if you don't, and you need to build a case for HR if he still doesn't respond and you need to move him out. Look, does some of this sound juvenile? Sure. But Slacker's antics are juvenile. If you can't beat him, join him.

STRATEGIES FOR MANAGING SLACKER

1   Find ways to objectively measure Slacker's productivity.

2   Set the minimum level of productivity bar higher than you would for most employees, because Slacker has the potential to achieve it, and he'll only deliver what you require of him.

3   Do your best to keep your cool with Slacker. He'll frustrate you with his untapped potential and ready excuses for poor performance. You need to be dispassionate when you put him on double-secret probation.

4   Keep good notes. You might need them for leverage or for a visit to HR.

Handling Miscues

Slacker will kick up countless miscues that you'll be forced to deal with. You need to handle Slacker firmly but unemotionally. Slacker is a bullshit artist, so he's not going to wilt when you blast him for missing a client appointment…he's going to come up with an excuse.

Like you do with an adolescent, you clearly lay out the consequences for Slacker's misbehavior, and then make sure you follow through on them. The worst thing for you is all the messes you'll need to clean up due to Slacker's irresponsibility. You will catch a fair amount of the shit (so will Slacker, but he won't care like you do), so you would be wise to find ways to have Slacker's miscues cause him pain.

WHAT YOU MIGHT DISCUSS WITH SLACKER

YOU: Hey, Slacker, where the hell were you this afternoon?

SLACKER: What do you mean?

YOU: I heard from McKenzie Oil. They said they had an appointment with you but you never showed.

SLACKER: Of course I showed. I stopped by there and the guy in the truck outside told me they were out all day and weren't coming back.

YOU: Didn't you go inside and ask for them? Clearly, he was wrong. I just spoke to McKenzie himself.

(CONTINUED ON FOLLOWING PAGE)

(CONTINUED)

SLACKER: Yeah, right, and have that driver think I thought he was lying? C'mon, Boss, that would have been pretty messed up.

YOU: What?!...And so where have you been all afternoon?

SLACKER: I had to go to another customer. They had an emergency.

YOU: Let me guess...

SLACKER (smirking): Yup, Smokey Hollow Country Club. They can't seem to get the right water pressure on the sprinklers off the first tee box. Boss, that's a real shit show over there. We have to make that right, or they just might leave us.

YOU: And I'm supposed to believe this. You're there three times a week. And no one from there ever called us about this problem.

SLACKER: Of course not. I own that relationship, Boss. When my clients have a problem, they call me first and I handle it.

YOU: Leave my office. Leave my office immediately.

Character Combinations with Slacker Worth Watching

- **FRANCHISE.** Franchise is the guy who wasn't born with Slacker's gifts but took what he was given and maximized it. Slacker's tendencies will frustrate Franchise, because Franchise would be godlike with Slacker's gifts and pedigree. Watch for rifts here, particularly if Slacker finds himself on a work team with Franchise.

- **ADHD BUTTERFLY.** Butterfly is a perfect partner in crime for Slacker, so watch for Slacker to make a run at enlisting Butterfly on his slacking escapades. Like the drunk at the bar who's trying to leave but gets sucked in by his drinking buddy who calls for "just one more," poor Butterfly will be powerless against Slacker's pull. Slacker offers everything Butterfly needs—companionship, escape from the norm and an unpredictably changing time together.

- **RETREAD.** Slacker and Retread share a couple of common traits. Both have bounced among many employers in their career and both look better on paper and in the interview seat than they do on the job. But Retread isn't as talented as Slacker, and couldn't possibly slack as well as Slacker. Plus, Retread doesn't pack the potential or pedigree of Slacker. You're ready to kick Retread to the curb the day she starts, but don't know how to rid yourself of her, whereas Slacker charms you with all that you think he could one day deliver, so you repeatedly resist the impulse to shoo him away, even if it might be for the best.

Keep or Throw Back?

The manager in you will want to retain Slacker. He's got the three Ps (polish, pedigree, and potential), after all. If you can't boost his performance, you're nothing. But at the end of the day, Slacker has too many hard-coded habits to easily break, so he will constantly disappoint. If you can get him to perform the minimum you need to see, maybe keeping him is more beneficial than the costs of throwing him back. But don't expect Slacker to step up and become a Franchise any time soon.

Character Profile #14

The Burnout

How Do You Know a Burnout When You See One?

He was flirting with Franchise status in the beginning of the Reagan administration. He was performing less admirably during the days that Clinton was asserting that he did not have sexual relations with *that woman*. And by the time U.S. troops failed to find any weapons of mass destruction and the Red Sox finally won a World Series, he was just barely pulling his own weight. He has become a fully formed Burnout.

There he dwells, several rungs down from a Franchise and a few more bad quarters away from the Retread's inevitable path straight to the door. You hope he either pulls it together or takes a hint, but neither seems to be happening any time soon.

Technology terrifies him. The new product line and pop culture references have passed him by, and if not for Eddie stopping by to reboot his terminal every time he hits the wrong button, Burnout would be staring at a blue screen all day long.

Starting Five

Utility Players

Benchwarmers

Trading Block Candidates

Simple statements like, "How do I send an e-mail?" or "What's my password again?" seem innocent enough if asked by Legend, and would be met with either a call to IT or you helping him personally. But when Burnout asks them, they're nails on a chalkboard, and wishes of seeing his resignation on your desk quickly compete with your recurring dreams of firing him.

His haircut, his attire, even his style of speech are all out of date and constant reminders to everyone that his best days are behind him.

Other than repayment for his past performance, you find yourself searching for a reason to keep him. Good luck.

THE BURNOUTS

WHY YOU LOVE 'EM	WHY YOU HATE 'EM
• They remind you of your Uncle Dick—no holiday meal is the same without them.	• They remind you of your Uncle Dick—who dominates family gatherings by speaking too much and too loudly about stories they've told you fifty times.
• They mean well.	• Just because someone means well doesn't mean that they don't suck.
• They don't have the energy to fight any major initiatives you want to push through.	• They don't have the energy for anything other than lunch.

Real-life/Screen Examples

- **Whitney Houston**—LOST: One of the greatest voices of her generation. FOUND: thousands of empty crack vials.

- **Willy Loman**—main character in *Death of a Salesman*.

- **Steven Segal in his last ten movies**—it's over, Steven…and please remove the ponytail.

A BURNOUT BEAUTY: WHITNEY HOUSTON

What the hell happened here? Whitney Houston can only be described as an extreme Burnout because of her precipitous fall from grace. At one point in the 1980s, this was one beautiful girl with one angelic voice.

Go ahead and blame Bobby Brown. Blame the crack cocaine. Blame her forgettable acting in *The Bodyguard*. But whatever the cause, it absolutely destroyed her.

Just look at her now. She appears on the occasional *60 Minutes* interview, swearing that she's found God and cleansed herself of the drugs that brought her career into the gutter alongside her. But then, almost on cue, a video of a performance surfaces in which she forgets the words, falls down on her face, and is so obviously intoxicated, she makes Paula Abdul look coherent.

There's this "point of no return" look to her that makes you wonder if even Whitney believes she can be restored to her former glory…or at least restore herself to some state of grace that would allow her to put herself out to pasture with some dignity intact. What a mess.

Ideal Settings

Burnout is in desperate need of a graceful path to pasture. He may respond to a new product line that reminds him of the "good old days," or by surrounding himself with a young, newbie team (where he can take on that feel-good Legend status, even if he was never really that good). The problem is that Burnout has seen it all, so finding that spark to reignite his interest could prove daunting to you. Moreover, Burnout often finds exhausting the very thought of embarking on efforts by managers to reinvigorate him. This might nudge Burnout closer to retirement rather than the intended consequence of igniting positive change. This may be a win/win. But the best bet for a pleasant Burnout sunset is finding a way to leverage his waning skills and breadth of experience by having him mentor or field train one of your team members. Allowing Burnout to train another, although risky, can be effective if restricted to tasks Burnout has mastered.

> *The best bet for a pleasant Burnout sunset is finding a way to leverage his waning skills and breadth of experience by having him mentor or field train one of your team members.*

Disastrous Settings

Burnout sends the wrong message—old, stagnant, and out of tune with the industry—to your account base. He dies in environments that quickly discard "old school" practices and practitioners for innovative ones. But Burnout can decline in environments that haven't changed for forty years as well. The manager who understands the strings to pull on her particular Burnout might at least slow the decline, and potentially tap the Legend that lies within. But simply permitting the Burnout to decline at the same old precipitous pace is an egregious error. In some cases, it may cause irreversible damage to your standing in the market. Nobody wants to see Burnout's slumped shoulders lumber through the door, no matter how strong he was in the past. Burnout is not who he once was, and allowing him to continue to bat cleanup when he should be an occasional pinch hitter will only cost you runs.

Training/Coaching/Monitoring

There will be few more frustrating and heartbreaking experiences than managing Burnout. There are only so many things you can do with him, and you're almost certain to see his performance decline further under your watch, no matter what magic you can conjure. Training and coaching are so unlikely to yield positive results, it should make you think twice about even trying to engage Burnout. Burnout shrugs a lot, and shakes his confused little head. It's painful for everyone involved.

The best bet for Burnout is periodic one-on-one supervision/quasi–life coaching sessions in which you gently nudge him toward retirement. Ask a lot of probing questions, listen your ass off, put on your best empathetic face, and pat him on the shoulder as Burnout walks out of your office.

STRATEGIES FOR MANAGING BURNOUT

1 Find something he's still good at (and likely to remain good at) and see if you can get him to do only that.

2 If he has a knack for training or mentoring, see if there's a Steady Eddie–type who might allow himself to be trained or mentored by Burnout.

(CONTINUED ON FOLLOWING PAGE)

Trading Block Candidates

3	See if you can get him to articulate an exit strategy. This will give you both something to look forward to, and will give you a sense of how long Burnout intends to stick around.
4	Keep him away from your Future and any somewhat promising newbies, because Burnout's negativity can have a tendency to spread like cancer, and you don't want Burnout's malignant cells invading the sterling young minds that you're trying desperately to mold.

Handling Miscues

It is important to remember that anyone who has had the long tenure that Burnout has endured is worthy of respect. Coworkers who see him treated in a way they perceive as unfair will begin to think that is how all employees are handled when they head out to pasture. So, as much as you would love to scream at him the next time he unintentionally deletes another critical e-mail, breathe deeply and remind others not to send Burnout critical e-mails.

Another group of people who are going to be watching how you and the company treat Burnout are those outside the company who have had, and continue to have, a relationship with Burnout. They give him business, respect, and admiration. Their relationship is personal, and mistreatment of Burnout will come back to haunt you in the form of no more business.

What You Might Discuss with Burnout

You: Hey, Burnout, you got a minute?

Burnout (sighing): Sure, kid. What can I do for you?

You: Well, I just got the quarterly numbers.

Burnout (sighing): Yeah, I about figured as much, kid. How'd they look?

You: Well, not quite as good as the quarter before, and quite a bit worse than the quarter before that. We seem to be moving in the wrong direction, B. Any thoughts about how to begin reversing the trend?

Burnout (sighing): I don't know. Times have changed, kid. The old magic doesn't quite work like it used to. Let's see … maybe I could dust off this old Rolodex and ring a few of my old customers and see if they'd be interested in any of the new stuff. That sure would be swell if they were.

You (sighing): Yeah, okay, B. I know a lot has changed since you began in the industry. Maybe you could … oh, look at that. Our time is up. So sorry, B. Look, let's both think about things you can do to get back on track, okay?

Character Combinations with Burnout Worth Watching

- **LEGEND.** Legend and Burnout are contemporaries, but they are rather different animals. Legend radiates distinction and class, while Burnout radiates stale beer and pretzels. If there is any way to splash cold water into Burnout's face, it may be to give him a healthy dose of what someone from his generation is still able to produce. The problem you'll have is that Legend has no respect for Burnout. Even in their best days, Burnout was no match for Legend.

- **WHISTLER.** This rat bastard is going to remind Burnout every chance he gets that he is not performing up to the levels of today's real performers. Whistler will be watching Burnout closely for slipups and laziness, and will never be afraid to call Burnout out to you. And as you're tailoring Burnout's sendoff package, watch out for leaked information to get to Whistler, who would jump at the chance to expose any special treatment you might be handing Burnout.

- **FUTURE.** Future will likely avoid Burnout all by himself, but please keep Burnout away from him. Burnout is anxious to tell about the time he met Tip O'Neill in the Dulles International Airport first-class lounge, or about that order of five-hundred-thousand Sony Walkman units he moved to Crazy Eddie's before Crazy Eddie really went "insane." With any luck, Future will find these stories tedious and run the hell away from Burnout.

Keep or Throw Back?

Listen, the writing is on the wall. Burnout is cooked and is well into his inevitable descent. Do yourself a favor and bail out before he takes you down with him.

Character Profile #15

The Retread

How Do You Know a Retread When You See One?

Retread is a tricky one to diagnose. At first glance, she's smooth and polished, as she describes her varied industry experience in broad, sweeping generalizations. When you first meet her, so many very exciting thoughts come to mind:

- Dressed like a pro... she's got to be successful.
- She knows more about this business than I do.
- Wow, she personally knows all the industry insiders.
- She can do anything! (She'll tell you this... over and over and over again.)
- What will it take for us to land her?

She plays herself off as a Legend dressed in Player's clothing, and one who is in extremely high demand. Retread trots out just enough industry jargon to convince you that she's an insider. If she were half as good at producing results as selling herself in an interview, Retread would be a perennial president's clubber. In an interview setting, you fall into her trap by failing to dig deeper into her checkered past.

Retread's biggest problem is that she sucks, but you don't realize it until she's in the door and collecting base pay and benefits. And if you're the one who hired her, you look like an asshole.

You see, the Retread is a nomad who leaves one job for another as soon as her bluff gets called. Retread changes jobs about as often as her underwear, and is impervious to blows to her unwavering self-confidence, no matter how misplaced it is. Retread leads with the surfacy self-confidence of Player, but she lacks Player's deep-in-the-bones assuredness (she might think she has it, but almost no one else does) and typically has enough life in her to clearly distinguish her from Burnout.

Despite her spotty track record at twenty prior companies, she massages her way in on the premise that business is business is business, and that yours is finally the opportunity she's been waiting for. On the day you extend that offer, the stars look perfectly aligned, and Retread—who alludes to twelve other offers she's juggling at once—jumps up to accept it (which should be your first clue that you just hired a Retread).

Soon after hire, Retread's glow begins to dim.

- You see the shoddy habits and generic techniques that help explain her checkered past.

- Retread's self-confidence wears thin, especially as you observe her ho-hum results and resistance (if not outright refusal) to incorporate feedback in your one-on-ones.

- Retread leads with excuses ("the market sucks," "the system is flawed," "we have the worst coffee and Danish in the industry," "everyone around me is an idiot") in a way that painfully reminds you of her well-rehearsed and, at the time, credible excuses she fed you during her job interview that overcame any objections about her countless job shifts.

What makes this all so maddening is that you actually fell for her pitch. And once you realize she's actually better selling herself in job interviews than at performing anything else, you get hit with that same nervous, hollow feeling you get when you see the police lights behind you when you've been cruising at 85 MPH.

Yes, you know Retread. You've worked with a million of them ... you just haven't worked with any one Retread for very long, because as soon as her cover gets blown, she bolts for the next opportunity.

Think we've been burned by Retread? You can bet your sweet ass we have. We just hope you do your homework on this chump so you don't fall victim yourself.

THE RETREADS

WHY YOU LOVE 'EM

- Best two days of a Retread manager's life: the day you hire them and the day you fire them.

- See above.

- See above.

WHY YOU HATE 'EM

- They snowed you into hiring them despite a spotty track record.

- They can't perform.

- They reject responsibility for everything.

Trading Block Candidates

Real-Life/Screen Examples

- **Don Imus**—Can you believe this angry, old, turkey-necked bag of hot wind is still on the air? Who listens to him?

- **Most NBA Coaches**—Can you believe Larry Brown still has a job? Oh, he is fired again? No. Wait. He was hired where?

- **Marion Barry**—Washington, D.C.'s former mayor who seemed to try to outdo himself with each successive drug- and prostitute-involved arrest.

A RADIO RETREAD: DON IMUS

Look, we've been listening to Don Imus since he was on WNBC radio in New York in the 1970s. Since then, the I-man has made a career of bouncing (or, more accurately, getting bounced) from radio station to radio station. This old bird has been hogging morning airwaves for years with quirky guests, painfully long diatribes about vaccination-induced autism, and periodic shock jock stunts that send advertisers to the exits and drive radio execs to can him.

Recently, Imus and his producer got caught in a controversy making disparaging on-air remarks about the Rutgers women's basketball team. Reverend Al Sharpton got in the mix, and the next thing you knew, Imus was sent packing again.

And just when you thought Imus was done for good, this old Retread resurfaces again on RFD-TV (a network built on the assumption that cattle auctions will drive viewership), and then leverages the thirty-five daily viewers he accumulated there to a new position on Fox Business, where he has now hoodwinked a vast network of radio affiliates into putting him on the air in their local markets—all of this without revamping a format that is now nearing forty years old. It just goes to show you that Retreads won't hold down a job for long, but they can always land another one right around the corner.

Ideal Setting

There are none. You will never get the promised results from Retread. In fact, to accurately forecast her performance, divide all of her estimates by a factor of 10. This is what we refer to as *The Retread Ratio*: 1 million dollars in forecasted savings or revenue growth is actually one hundred thousand dollars;

- A reported ten-page order is, in reality, a one-pager; and
- If she claims to have spent fifty hours a week working on a project, it is closer to five.

Disastrous Settings

Quite possibly all work environments are ill-suited for Retread. If you have a Retread on your team, and have ineffective mechanisms in place to document all her screwups, she will stay on longer than

Trading Block Candidates

she should, add considerably to your list of headaches, and steadily erode any credibility you had with upper management. Taking her at her word, paying her what she purports to be worth, and wasting a substantial period of time waiting for Retread's bullshit to turn into gold dust is a career suicide mission.

Training/Coaching/Monitoring

Retread is the queen of excuses, and she's good at engaging others to listen to them. With Retread, you need to clearly state what you expect in terms of performance results. Track her metrics closely, state plainly the objective gaps between current and desired states, and then gather comparative data across the company, the region, and your team. Choose the numbers that minimize Retread's wiggle room. You need to start building the case for her inevitable pink slip.

STRATEGIES FOR MANAGING RETREAD

| Cut your losses and fire them.

Handling Miscues

Your biggest challenge with Retread is not losing your shit. Her path to making you look bad was paved the day she convinced you to hire her. Now that she's here, and you see what she's really made of, you want to choke her for every little thing she does. Resist the urge.

Police vigilantly. Give her constructive feedback like you would anyone else. And document everything. Best to own this mistake as soon as you recognize it...it will help you make your case sooner and stronger, as Retread has likely been down the HR highway more times than you have.

WHAT YOU MIGHT DISCUSS WITH RETREAD

YOU: Hey, Retread, you told me you were going to have those three reports to me this week.

RETREAD: Really? No, I told you I was only going to have one. I told you I could possibly deliver three, but that was before daylight saving time arrived, and so I lost that extra hour this week.

YOU: Daylight saving? Have you lost your freaking mind?

RETREAD: Hey, I have no control over the clock.

YOU: What?! Wait, forget about three reports, you didn't even deliver one this week.

RETREAD: Yes, I did.

YOU: No, you didn't.

RETREAD: I definitely delivered one report this week. I submitted it on Tuesday. Tammy in service must have processed it wrong again. She always does that.

YOU: Can you call Tammy right now while I'm here so we can get it processed correctly?

(CONTINUED ON FOLLOWING PAGE)

(*CONTINUED*)

RETREAD: I could, but Tammy just left on a three-month sailing sabbatical around the world. I won't be able to reach her. I bet that report is lost forever now. Man, that sucks.

YOU: Sucks? I'll tell you what sucks, you little piece of...

Please note: All conversations with Retread have the possibility of degenerating like this. Breathe deeply. Count to ten. Sing the chorus of "One Headlight" by The Wallflowers to yourself to cool off. She will work you hard at every turn. Document well and stay cool!

Character Combinations with Retread Worth Watching

- **THE SLACKER.** Slacker is looking for corners to cut, and Retread has made a career out of corner cutting. The difference here is that Slacker actually has the potential to produce, and does from time to time. Slacker just doesn't produce consistently enough. Retread has a nose for recruitable hooky mates and has excuses at her disposal to share. If you ever want to see Slacker establish himself as a consistent performer, keep these two apart until you can unload Retread.

- **THE LEGEND.** Legend will spot Retread's bullshit from a mile away. Therefore, in order to protect his impeccable reputation, expect Legend to avoid Retread at all costs. This is fine for you, as you don't want Legend's rep tarnished any more than he does, but it might be worth having Legend around during a team meeting to watch Legend cut down Retread in front of everyone for making an unfounded sweeping generalization about the industry.

- **THE BURNOUT.** Burnout and Retread are the sweat hogs of any team. They both completely suck. Retread will frequently saddle up next to Burnout, as that's about as favorable a comparison as she can get. Burnout would move away, if only he weren't so damn tired.

Keep or Throw Back?

If you are okay with 10 percent of Retread's projections actually turning into tangible, viable results, then keep her aboard, because that is all—if even that—you are going to get from this con. But that's not what we recommend. In case we haven't already made abundantly clear, let us tell you straight up: shake yourself loose of this phony time-sucker as soon as humanly possible. Toss her overboard!

Character Profile #16

The Asshole

How Do You Know an Asshole When You See One?

This guy walks the halls like he's the man, takes the head seat in the conference room, and insists on the office with the best view. He's the arrogant, obnoxious, over-entitled douche bag that nobody can stand. Asshole suits himself one of the guys, but all of the guys talk about him behind his back. Just as every village has its idiot, every workplace has its Asshole.

Assholes come in one of three varieties:

1. **Type A—Associative Asshole.** This is Badass without the results, Player without the looks, and Noodler with the wrong information. A real bastard who, if not for your own inability to fill his slot with someone better, would be gone in a heartbeat. He parks too close every morning and never flushes the toilet. An Associative A-hole wants recognition for value like his more successful peers, but he doesn't add any and isn't worthy of it.

2. **Type B—Born-Better Asshole.** This category is mainly reserved for the guy "born better" than most of us. He has the status, family name, and background to succeed anywhere. The missing ingredient? Brains and/or work ethic. He saunters into the workplace like he's walking onto his dad's forty-foot yacht. He's doing us a favor just by allowing us to be associated with him. He's so vain, he probably thinks this book (particularly the part about Franchise) is about him. We know your pain, Carly Simon. We know your pain.

3. **Type C—Cantankerous Asshole.** This jerkoff is insensitive to all that takes place around him. He asks about a coworker's son who he knows failed out of college or just missed a shot at the buzzer for the state championship. He pontificates on the horrors of resorting to military force, knowing his coworker in the cubicle next door has a son in Iraq. CA didn't acquire his asshole-ness through osmosis (like Associative Asshole) or inherit it (like Born-Better Asshole). CA's asshole behavior is learned through a long history of abuse.

THE ASSHOLES

WHY YOU LOVE 'EM

- You don't. No one does. It's okay.

WHY YOU HATE 'EM

- They're selfish, demanding, and entitled.
- They belittle others.
- They routinely send nasty-gram e-mails...to their mother.

Real-life/Screen Examples

- **O.J. Simpson**—everyone knows this man was lucky to avoid prison the first time. But he ended up there eventually. Karma sucks.

- **Mike Francesca**—what entitles this know-it-all, sports-radio talker to treat his callers like they're no-bodies?

- **Simon Cowell**—drove thousands of hopeful American Idol participants to tears with gratuitous insults about everything from their singing ability to their hairdos.

- **Kanye West**—What would have happened if Kanye had stolen the stage and award show limelight from Snoop Dog and his posse instead of Taylor Swift. Our guess? It would have looked like a "shank scene" out of the HBO jailhouse series "Oz."

A COURT-CERTIFIED ASSHOLE: O.J. SIMPSON

The life of Orenthal James Simpson is a perfect example of someone falling recklessly from revered athlete into pure asshole status.

O.J. has never taken any responsibility for anything he's done wrong, and expects the world to roll over for him because at one point in his life he could fly across a football field. He was given a handful of roles in television commercials and major motion pictures even though he couldn't act. He was heralded as one of the greatest athletes of his generation. He seemingly had it all. So what did he do?

Just (allegedly) brutally murdered two people—one being the mother of his children—in a jealous rage, hired a legal defense dream team, got acquitted, swore to find the "real killers," and then was found liable for the wrongful death of Nicole Brown Simpson and Ronald Goldman.

He sulked about his "mistreatment" and yet went about his life playing golf and retreating to Florida to protect his remaining assets. Then, as if he had forgotten what it was like to be on trial for his life, he committed an armed robbery in Las Vegas in an attempt to get back some of his memorabilia. He got arrested all over again, went to trial all over again, and got the thirty or so years he should have received the first time. To add even more capital to his Asshole portfolio, he wrote a book describing how he would have killed Nicole had he done it.

O.J., without question, is an Asshole.

Ideal Settings

An ideal setting would be Asshole rehab. Unfortunately, no such thing exists, and if it did your company wouldn't pay for it, so good luck finding a place for this loudmouth malcontent within the context of your workplace. If you can't get rid of him, then find a way for this belligerent jerk to telecommute and do it fast.

Disastrous Settings

Keep him far away from customer service or any other client-facing position. We would not recommend him for an HR post. Really, any place where Asshole might be forced to interact meaningfully with others should be avoided.

Training/Coaching/Monitoring

You can't train, coach, or monitor Asshole…you can only hope to contain him. Good luck.

STRATEGIES FOR MANAGING ASSHOLE

1	Asshole speaks Asshole-ese…don't be afraid to hit this guy first and right between the eyes.
2	Protect your real keepers from Asshole.
3	Look for the right opportunity to remove him, position yourself well, and move on it.

Handling Miscues

Hold him accountable. Keep careful notes. Consult with HR. Build the file. Look for an opportunity he gives you to swiftly move him out.

WHAT YOU MIGHT DISCUSS WITH ASSHOLE

YOU: Asshole, did you really show Steady Eddie your pay stub? You know you make more than he does, and now I've got to pick up the pieces here.

ASSHOLE: Well, he was telling me about the new car he was buying and acting like he was a big shot. So I thought I would show him who was boss.

YOU: Hey Asshole, I'm the boss. And I know Eddie, and there is no way he was acting like a big shot. It's not in his DNA.

ASSHOLE: Funny...because from my vantage point, all you do is sit around here and push paper all day. Still wondering why they're paying you at all. I'm the only productive guy in this damn place.

YOU: Funny...because I was just looking at the quarterly results, and I'm seeing you just nosed out Burnout last quarter. Not sure I'd be playing the productivity card, Asshole.

ASSHOLE: Yeah, well this company sucks, and so do you.

Character Combinations with Asshole Worth Watching

- **NOODLER:** Just to get under Noodler's skin, Asshole will make bold, sweeping claims with nothing to back them up. He'll challenge Noodler's well-reasoned arguments and publicly call into question the integrity of his research. Things get really interesting if Asshole ever gets his hands on proof that Noodler actually made a mistake.

- **NEEDY NED:** Asshole will feed on Ned's insecurities. He'll tell Ned that his inexperience costs the company millions. He'll warn Ned that there is a new product line coming that will require expertise that Ned doesn't have. He'll turn the lights off when he knows Ned is in the bathroom all by himself.

- **BURNOUT:** Asshole gets giddy just thinking about Burnout's missteps, and calls him out when his tie is too wide, his shoes are too scuffed or his presentations seem outdated. Any chance Asshole gets to hammer home the fact that Burnout is in the twilight of his career, he takes.

Keep or Throw Back?

Get this chump off your squad. Your team's success depends on it.

PART III
THE TEAMS

An Overview

So you've got your people pegged. You know you've got a Badass, a Slacker and a Needy Ned, and you're armed with some strategies for getting more productivity from each of those individuals. So what more do you need?

Well, you're more than just a private, individual coach for the various people who report to you. You're a manager. This collection of individuals is connected to you as part of a *team*. And when they come together, dynamics happen—jealousies rage, sparks fly, synergies become possible, and team identity solidifies or falls apart.

In this section of the book, you conduct a thorough inventory of your team's talent and see how the various flavors mix together. See what spices you need to add or neutralize.

In the pages that follow, we profile and analyze five classic types of teams. The point of the analysis is to demonstrate how you as a manager can get more from your team by modifying certain team policies and reallocating your time depending on your team makeup.

The five classic teams are:

1 The Dream Team

The Dream Team doesn't need much explanation. This is a collection of superstars that will make you the envy of your peers. In the language of this book, it's a team of Starters. They will make you rich and your company famous as long as you don't screw it up. But even this group of studs warrants a thorough team analysis. How do you keep their egos in check? Is the competition too cutthroat? Since any drop-off in performance will be deemed your failure, there is limited upside and big downside career risk.

2 Hickory

Remember the 1980s basketball movie Hoosiers? (If you haven't seen it, put this book down immediately, rent it, and watch it. Seriously, do it now—we'll wait.) The small Indiana high school team, Hickory, had only one bona fide star on its roster: Jimmy Chitwood. Jimmy was Hickory's Franchise, surrounded by Utility Players and Benchwarmers, who found a way to take his team to the state championship. The trick to managing a team like Hickory is getting the Utility Players and Benchwarmers to buy into their roles and leveraging their unique strengths, while making Franchise feel special.

All Thumbs 3

We all like our thumbs...they're an essential part of our hands that help us function. But if you had all thumbs, you might never actually get anything done. This is the team of Utility Players without a Starter to be found. How do you get these thumbs to produce consistently?

Wounded Veterans 4

The Wounded Vets are the tenured and tired. They talk longingly of the old days before e-mail and the Internet. Their previous manager treated them like beloved old circus elephants, and so they have become quite the entitled, underperforming bunch. Can you turn this ship around? Do you need to shake them up or inject some life?

The Rookies 5

The Rookies are the fresh crop of recent college kids who are packed with energy, a love of partying, and very little understanding of what it takes to succeed at your company. You want to shape these eager young minds from the beginning, and sort out the talented (think Futures) from the merely energetic. You institute structure and oversight and strict adherence to work activity requirements. The Rookies are fun but an awful lot of work.

NOTE

We fully recognize there are more than five types of teams in the world. The ones we discuss in this book are classics that should be familiar to you. The key here is for you to be able to assess and tailor a unique management strategy for each specific team you manage. The analysis of the five team profiles that follows will prepare you for that.

Our analysis for each team includes the following:

- **Who's on the team?** If you don't know what we're talking about then you haven't read Parts I and II yet, and that really pisses us off. Go back and read it now. Seriously, read it. After doing so, you should have a solid understanding of every player on your team. You know not only what their character types are but also their tenure, idiosyncrasies, strengths and weaknesses, industry knowledge, and power positions on the team.

- **What's in it for you?** Taking on almost any kind of team presents potential upside and downside. Others around you know your players and their work history. Armed with this information, you don't need a statistics degree to project future performance. In each case, if that team performs beyond or below expectations, you are likely to be given credit or blame.

- **What can you reasonably expect?** Table your wildest fantasies for a moment and determine what you could reasonably expect from this team once you put your management magic to work. How have they performed historically, and with some strategic interventions by you, how significantly can you hope to move the needle forward?

- **What will team dynamics look like?** We want you to understand how the players interact with each other as a group. What are the power dynamics? Who can sway the group? In our analysis of the teams below, we'll give representative verbal exchanges among team members that will highlight what we want you to look for.

- **How can you maximize your time?** For the Rookies, you'll be spending much of your time policing and training, while for the Dream Team, you'll be spending your time kissing their asses so they continue performing and tuning out headhunter calls. Each team will require you to allocate your time differently in order to maximize productivity.

- **Special Policy Considerations:** We're often struck by the flexibility given to managers everywhere, even in traditional corporate settings, to shape their own team policies. Sure, senior executives require certain behaviors from the entire company, but managers are largely left on their own to determine whether one or more team members must:

1. Attend routine team meetings or trainings;
2. punch in and out at the beginning and end of each workday;
3. get manager approval before making pricing or expense decisions; and

4.   subject themselves to weekly individual meetings
     with you.

We encourage you to consider reshaping your team policies to capitalize on the team makeup and interpersonal dynamics you're likely
to find.

Team #1

The Dream Team

Who's on the Team?

Think about Magic Johnson, Larry Bird, Michael Jordan, Patrick Ewing, and Charles Barkley all playing for the same team. They were a collection of superstars who carried their respective NBA teams on their backs during the season—and here they were competing together for a gold medal on the 1992 U.S. Basketball Team. How easy was that team to coach? An idiot could lead them to the title, right? Not so fast.

At first glance, inheriting a team of stars is a manager's fast track to the C-suite. You know you're sitting on a Dream Team when you are loaded with Starters. You have to distinguish among your several Franchise players. This squad has no dead weight—no Burnout, no Retread, not even a benchwarmer like Slacker. Others stare in awe at the Dream Team. In the cafeteria, people vie for adjacent table space, in hopes that by just sitting in close proximity, they will absorb Dream Team's talent through osmosis. Secretly, they all want to get an invite to play for you alongside them.

What's in It for You?

The upside to inheriting the Dream Team is obvious. These corporate superstars can carry you to greatness. They're certainly not going to let any manager get in the way of their success. Because of their uncompromising ambition, the worst they're going to perform is usually pretty damn well.

On the downside, if for some reason the Dream Team falters, everyone from upper management to the all-stars themselves are going to be pointing their fingers at you. Like an underachieving professional sports team, no one will be questioning the frontline talent… they will be questioning the manager, and after just a little underachieving, they will be calling for your head.

> *The upside to inheriting the Dream Team is obvious. These corporate superstars can carry you to greatness. They're certainly not going to let any manager get in the way of their success…. On the downside, if for some reason the Dream Team falters, everyone from upper management to the all-stars themselves are going to be pointing their fingers at you.*

In addition, any Dream Team is typically loaded with outsized personalities and demanding sorts who expect you to be falling all over yourself to be serving them. They will compete ferociously for your time and attention in a way that will cause you to often give one or more less of your energy than they think they deserve.

What Can You Reasonably Expect?

The Dream Team thrives when the stars are spending most of the time doing what they're best at, and off-loading on someone (i.e., you) those things they hate doing (i.e., paperwork, battling upper management for more resources, taking on battles across departments to facilitate productivity). In a perfect world, Dream Teamers bring distinct skills and they get rewarded (publicly or monetarily) for sharing those skills and leveraging those of each other. This reduces unproductive competition, and increases the likelihood that the whole will exceed the sum of its parts.

What Will Team Dynamics Look Like?

Dream Team dynamics range wildly from idyllic to nightmarish. Infighting among Dream Teamers is legendary, and typically originates from competing egos not getting enough massaging. Look, these guys are accustomed to being superstars, and superstar treatment can only be granted to so many players. If you don't devote enough attention to getting enough kudos and benefits to each Dream Teamer, you will end up pissing some of them off, and then falling victim to mass exodus or mass sabotage of team results. Turf wars are common, so role definition and clear communication of allocated responsibility is paramount. The last thing you want is Legend bitching about Player hogging the mic during the pep rally segment of the company picnic.

Remember, after the 1992 Olympics, subsequent "dream teams" failed to win the gold medal until 2008. You could argue that the quality of the talent fell short of the 1992 gold standard, but you could also safely conclude that the coaches of those teams failed to keep egos and self-interest in check. Suddenly, USA Basketball found recruiting America's best players had become more challenging. In 2008, Duke University head coach Mike Krzyzewski, widely recognized as the master of star player manipulation, was able to sell the idea of a new-and-improved Dream Team to the NBA's best, and then used his wiles to balance playing time and scoring without sacrificing team success. As a result, the gold medal returned to the United States, where it belonged.

How Can You Maximize Your Time?

Managing the Dream Team can be exhausting. One school of thought is to back the hell out of the way and let them do their thing. The problem with that is that the Dream Teamers' competing egos will crash into each other and send the infighting to problematic levels. We're not suggesting you hover over them and constrain their productivity. We are, however, recommending that you take the time to determine each Dream Teamer's specific wants and desires, and then race like crazy to make sure they're met (all the while opportunistically reminding each Dream Teamer what you're doing to meet them). You always want Dream Teamers to recognize the value you bring, even if it's merely removing corporate obstacles so they can perform.

Dream Teamers like a challenge, so you need to push the bar just high enough for them to reach their goals. This can help them achieve their full potential.

Special Policy Considerations:

- **LOVE THEM EQUALLY, BUT DIFFERENTLY:** When you're managing the Dream Team, you don't have one Franchise—you have four of them. If you treat them identically, you risk making them feel ordinary (arguably the worst feeling any Franchise can experience), and therefore underappreciated. You'll need to think creatively about finding Franchise-specific perks that appeal to each, without making any of them feel as though another's set of perks is more desirable than their own. So the balancing act for you is not only ensuring equality and specificity, but also effectively communicating player-specific perks and selling their relative equality.

- **LEVERAGE SKILLS:** Most teams have some inherent level of interdependence. That is, the success of the team relies on the cooperation of the players on it. (Note that there are some exceptions to this, of course. For example, most Dream Team sales teams can thrive without too much cooperation among the various players.) What you'll need to think carefully about is building in incentives for each of the Dream Teamers to share his skill set with the rest of the team. The only way this will work is if each Dream Teamer feels as though the others are contributing equally. If one gets the sense another is holding back to protect his own interests, or to somehow distinguish himself from the pack, then you can have a severe backlash that causes tensions at best, and mass departures (including yours) at worst.

Dream Team
Water Cooler Chatter

LEGEND (yawning): I'm exhausted.

FRANCHISE: Are you, old timer? You must be getting old. I think I could go all night.

PLAYER: Legend, you do look awful. You need to get yourself a nap, you poor little thing. Future, honey, can you make yourself useful and go get one of those lattes for Legend?

BADASS: I am the balls. I never get tired. Fatigue is for the weak.

FUTURE: Um . . . a latte? Make myself useful?

BADASS: What she means, towel boy, is that you can't carry our jock straps, and you might as well stop choking on our dust and add some value. Legend isn't exactly blowing it out either, but with a little hit of caffeine, maybe he can pick up the phone and make some useful introductions. You, on the other hand...

LEGEND: Now wait a minute. If I had all the perks you had, Badass, I'd be the MVP. Back when I was a kid like you, there was no such thing as a hard drive, and faxes came on that awful rolled-up paper.

FRANCHISE: Look, old man. I can't speak for Badass, but I get what I get because I am the person they come to when they need to come to somebody.

PLAYER: Oh, you're the man, all right, Franchise. How else could we explain why Boss sucks on your toes during our team meetings?

BADASS: Hey Player, at least Franchise produces instead of flitting around to his little "constituencies" all the time.

PLAYER: My constituencies are our company's biggest clients, you big, blustery buffoon! The only reason they're still with us is because they like me. I should be in the company hall of fame for retaining them as clients.

LEGEND (yawning): I gotta go. This really is exhausting.

FUTURE: I guess I'll go get that latte.

Team #2

Hickory

Who's on the Team?

In *Hoosiers*, Jimmy Chitwood was the best high school basketball player in the state of Indiana. And once he decided to bail out Coach Norman Dale and join the team mid-season, his role-playing teammates fell right in behind him, fed him the ball on nearly every possession, ran the picket fence play, and watched him score. Jimmy put the team and Coach Dale on his back and marched them to the state championship.

The Hickory team is easy to spot—look for the stud surrounded by a bunch of hapless no-names. It's Franchise at the front, with Utility Players and Benchwarmers tagging along. Every industry has its example of the 80/20 rule... but on Hickory, it's more like 95/5. Just as Jimmy did for Hickory, the Franchise can single-handedly carry his team (and you) to greatness.

What's in It for You?

The upside of inheriting a Hickory team is that no one really expects much from anyone other than Franchise. If you get some pop out of the Utility Players, look out…you could be headed for a huge promotion. The risk is that you don't sufficiently help Franchise and he leaves, or for some reason his performance drops off, in which case the blood is on *your* hands.

What Can You Reasonably Expect?

Team Hickory is at its best when Franchise is happy and he likes his teammates. A happy Franchise lets you worry less about warding off headhunters and more about clearing the way for him to get his stuff done. And when Franchise likes his team, he's more likely to share best practices, let teammates sit in on important meetings, and consult with them on their ongoing issues. If you can get Franchise to transfer his knowledge, then you can really create something special.

> *Everything centers on Franchise….He gets all the credit for Hickory's success and receives entitlements that others do not. If he fails, you and your entire team fail. So Hickory will either be in harmony or it won't, depending entirely on whether the Utility Players and Benchwarmers can tolerate the perks Franchise receives.*

What Will Team Dynamics Look Like?

This one's easy. Everything centers on Franchise. Remember, at the end of the day, you work for Franchise, not the other way around. He gets all the credit for Hickory's success and receives entitlements that others do not. If he fails, you and your entire team fail. So Hickory will either be in harmony or it won't, depending entirely on whether the Utility Players and Benchwarmers can tolerate the perks Franchise receives for being, well, Franchise. If you've got a disgruntled Burnout or underperforming Player, look out, because both are adept at building reality show–style coalitions that could undermine Hickory's success.

How Can You Maximize Your Time?

As Hickory's manager, you've got two major tasks: keeping Franchise productive and happy, and soothing any resentment from the others. In order to do that, you need to split your time between facilitating Franchise's business and strategically adding value to the others to remind them that they're important in their own right.

Special Policy Considerations:

- **FRANCHISE FORGIVENESS FACTOR (A.K.A. THE 'JORDAN RULES'):** For many years, Michael Jordan received preferential treatment from his coach, Phil Jackson, which became known as the "Jordan Rules." Jordan was allowed to miss practices, travel on road trips separate from the rest of the team, and even call plays for himself during timeouts. Giving Franchise comparable treatment on your team—such as allowing him to miss team meetings, and having someone else (you) tackle his administrative tasks—is what we call the Franchise Forgiveness Factor.

  As an example, let's say you have a standing policy about getting to team meetings on time, and ADHD Butterfly strolls in from the break room ten minutes after your meeting was scheduled to begin. You ask to speak with him after the meeting, and you blow a gasket. Then, next week Franchise also strolls in from the break room ten minutes late. You wave to Franchise and indicate that his tardiness is no problem at all.

  Deplorable, right? Flatly unfair! Well, maybe. But look, if you had someone of Michael Jordan's caliber on your team and he came to tell you that he was leaving for a competitor who promised to let him craft his own schedule and avoid the routine of team meetings that added no material value to him, you'd burst into tears and never forgive yourself.

Your challenge is not deciding whether to grant Franchise Forgiveness (you really have no choice), but stating the specifics of your policy and the rationale behind it clearly to everyone on Team Hickory. Make it clear to all—including Franchise—that Franchise gets Forgiveness for achieving a certain level of performance. Also, state emphatically and often that, (1) if anyone else achieves the stated performance, he, too, will enjoy Franchise Forgiveness, and (2) once Franchise dips below the level, he will be subject to the same dreary shit everyone else is.

And please be on the lookout for Scottie Pippen (read: a Badass, Player, or Future), who might be very good and command some favorable treatment from you but is certainly no Michael Jordan. You work for Franchise, but you really don't work for Pippen.

One more point on this. You don't want to rub the Franchise Forgiveness Factor in the others' faces. Most of them have no chance of getting these benefits, but you still need their steady production. You may consider giving each person on Team Hickory a separate, personally relevant perk for achieving something that's within his reach.

- **GETTING SOMETHING BACK FROM FRANCHISE:** A more interesting challenge is getting Franchise to deliver favors for you, like allowing up-and-coming Utility Players to work side by side with him, and orchestrating a team training led by Franchise on some technical subjects. The Franchise will always deliver results. But if you can also get him to transfer any of his knowledge to the other Hickory members, then you've really pulled off a trick.

In order to do that, you need leverage. In order to get leverage, you need to deliver value to Franchise that he ultimately can't live without. Once *you* identify that, you can dangle it (or the threat of removing it) in front of him to get something in return.

Hickory
Water Cooler Chatter

WHISTLER: So I understand Boss is sleeping with Franchise.

MR. INAPPROPRIATE: You think she's bangin' him? Oh, I've got to hear this.

NEEDY NED: Why him? Why not me? Oh, that's so unfair.

NOODLER: On what basis are you making this claim, Whistler? I need HARD facts.

PLAYER: It must be true. Why else would Boss be doing all Franchise's paperwork and letting him skip our team meeting every week?

WHISTLER: Shhh! Here comes Franchise!

PLAYER: Hey Franchise, how you doing, baby? Looking good, sugar...looking real good! Look at this stud, y'all.

FRANCHISE: Yeah...hi.

WHISTLER: What brings you here, Franchise?

FRANCHISE: My thirst...this *is* a water cooler.

NOODLER: Franchise, we need to know: Why does Boss treat you better than she treats the rest of us?

FRANCHISE: Well, as she always says, I've been the top producer in the region for the past four years, so she handles some of my paperwork and she doesn't need to know my location every ten minutes. She wants me spending most of my time producing, which is what I do best.

NEEDY NED: But does she ever hug you?

FRANCHISE: Oh shit, I gotta go … big call this afternoon.

MR. INAPPROPRIATE: So wait … are they doing it or what?

WHISTLER: Mr. I, you are such a pig.

Team #3

All Thumbs

Who's on the Team?

The All Thumbs team is one littered with Utility Players—Noodlers, Steady Eddies, Doers, and Whistlers. There's nothing inherently wrong with a couple of thumbs. In fact, without them, our hands would not be able to complete most routine tasks. You would get by well enough without one of your other fingers. You could manage without the pointer (though picking your nose would be an issue). You would avoid unnecessarily escalating road rage incidents without the middle. You could do everything but marry without your ring finger. And pinky? That puny digit is basically a leftover from some evolutionary oversight. It's of no use whatsoever, unless you're a dainty tea drinker. But if all of your fingers were thumbs, you'd be screwed. How the hell would you get anything done? How would you complete even the most basic tasks? Typing? Writing? Waving? Could you ever get them to function like a normal hand? This is your challenge.

What's in It for You?

When you're sitting around the conference table taking stock of your All Thumbs team, the pessimist in all of us would let despair consume us. This is not an impressive lot. Where is your performance going to come from? The upside here is that you come off as a management genius if you get anything solid out of these guys. The downside is that you have no dependable performer, so you either need to go out and recruit one, develop one, or somehow get these guys to work together in such a way that they outperform. When you have the All Thumbs team, you need to let your superiors know it so you can head off any criticism of your management ability (and take credit in the event you can actually get them to work well).

> This is not an impressive lot. Where the hell is your performance going to come from? The upside here is that you come off as a management genius if you get anything out of these guys. The downside is that you have no dependable performer, so you either need to go out and recruit one, develop one, or somehow get these guys to work together in such a way that they outperform.

What Can You Reasonably Expect?

Be realistic. The All Thumbs will never blow the doors off. They just don't have it in their genetic makeup. You want to nudge these guys forward by expanding their skills, exposing them to sound training and mentors, giving them lots of encouragement (when warranted)—and alternatively good-natured kicks in the ass (when warranted)—and making sure you know them each well enough to steer them into tasks that match their strengths. If they are doing things they're good at, then they are most likely to maximize performance.

What Will Team Dynamics Look Like?

This is a group lacking confidence. They don't feel particularly good about themselves because nothing they've ever done would warrant particularly high self-esteem. So the dynamics are remarkably un-remarkable. Don't anticipate a lot of jockeying to be lead dog. Don't expect a lot of unreasonable demands for special, performance-based treatment. Don't look for ego-driven turf wars. If you want dynamics, you'll need to shake the trees. Press them for results. Nudge them out of their comfort zones. Ask aloud who on this team is going to step up and fill the performance void.

How Can You Maximize Your Time?

Because the Thumbs are so reactive in nature, you'll need to find creative ways to infuse energy and build excitement. You'll want to lean heavily on team meetings with loud music and fancy Power-Point presentations. In your one-on-ones, spend considerable time wrestling out of each Thumb what he particularly likes to do and considers strengths of his. Thumbs are so passive, you will have to pull information out of them, and guard against letting them say what they think you want to hear. The better you know your Thumbs, the more likely you are to extract success.

Special Policy Considerations:

- **BIG REWARD FOR BIG PERFORMANCE:** This is the crowd that got straight Cs in college. Their mo-dus operandi is to shoot squarely for the middle of the pack and land there in anonymity. One way to get them to think more ambitiously is to pull together a contest that heavily rewards big perfor-mance. What's the worst case? Either no one steps up, and you're no worse than you were before insti-tuting thE CONTEst, or you stir a little life into them, and a couple of Thumbs go at each other's throats to

try and win the contest. Would a little Thumb wrestling really be the worst thing in the world? Hell no!

- **TRACKING ACTIVITY:** Because of their satisfaction with mediocrity and comfort with passivity,
  you should take a close look at how the Thumbs are
  spending their days. Think carefully about what behavior you want to see from each Thumb AND HAVE
  each take on a customized weekly "activity chart"
  with each activity weighted for its relative importance. Childish? Yes. Micromanagement? Sure. But
  look, Thumbs are sheep, and their desperate need
  for a shepherd warrants this kind of thing from you.
  If you don't lead them, no one will.

All Thumbs
Water Cooler Chatter

STEADY EDDIE (quietly, as if in a church pew): Good morning,
everyone.

NOODLER: Is it good?…what makes it good? I have at least
three pieces of evidence for why it's bad.

DOER (racing past): Hi, everyone. Would love to chat, but I
have a to-do list a mile long.

WHISTLER: I really have no clue what Doer does all day other
than race around and complain about all she has to do.
I'm gonna catch that little bullshitter one of these days.

STEADY EDDIE (as if he were stricken with laryngitis): I think
Doer is doing just fine…. Such wonderful weather we're
having, wouldn't you agree?

YOU (passing by with Doer in tow)**:** Hey, I thought I might run into my team here. What's everyone up to?

EVERYONE: (Silence, eyes cast downward, sipping water.)

YOU: Right, that's what I thought. How about an impromptu meeting right now?

DOER: Love to, Boss, but I should get going. I have mountains to climb before the end of day. Literally, mountains to climb.

YOU: Doer, I think your "free the prisoners" letter-writing campaign can wait. Hey, we've got to have a big week, team. We'll be having our quarterly reviews coming up in the next two weeks, and we've been sluggish, even for us.

NOODLER: Define sluggish, Boss.

YOU: Well, in your case, Noodler, sluggish can best be defined by twisting yourself in a knot over basic shit that most normal people handle in minutes, but for some reason, it takes you weeks. You've turned around just two of the fifteen agreements that came to you for revision and signature. Two agreements, Noodler. Two. In one freaking quarter. That's sluggish.

WHISTLER: Well said, Boss. It's about time you let Noodler have it. That is long overdue.

YOU: Whistler, you're another one. You have your head so far up HR's ass—and yes, you can tell them I said this—that you're neglecting your real job, which, as far as I can tell is getting things done, not busting your peers for handbook violations. I'm serious, team. I need performers. And I need them now. Am I clear?

EVERYONE: (Silence, eyes cast downward, sipping water.)

YOU: Good. I hope so.

Team #4

Wounded Veterans

Who's on the Team?

Oh, what a pathetic lot these Wounded Veterans are. You look around the conference room and all you see are a bunch of tired, old, embittered losers who have spent the latter part of their careers consuming the company's resources, contributing just enough to keep their jobs, and ripping through managers as if it were an Olympic event. All you hear are stories about the good old days, when money was made in spite of their ineptitude, slothful habits, and bad work ethic.

These Retreads, Burnouts, and Slackers band together like long-lost blood brothers, lunch together as if it were the Last Supper, and are rumored to have hooked themselves on cigarettes for the sole purpose of justifying more breaks during the workday. These chumps are long on institutional knowledge and excuses, but low on just about anything positive.

What's in It for You?

When someone shouts, "Dead man walking!" as you walk in to commence your first team meeting, it should strike you that managing the Wounded Vets is not a winning proposition. You're inheriting a pack of professional con artists who are in cahoots to see that you fail just like the long line before you. Their long tenure must carry significant weight among senior management (nothing else could explain why they're still around), so merely bellyaching to your boss is not likely to change much. Obviously, if you could turn these turds around, you would be appointed to some presidential committee on management, but that's about as likely as Jessica Simpson obtaining a teaching post at Harvard. Your best bet is to usher in a bold new era of discipline and accountability, and start driving them out, one bad apple at a time.

What Can You Reasonably Expect?

While no one expects much from you when you take on the Wounded Vets, rest assured that you won't be given a free pass if you, like the long lines before you, fail. This assignment is distinct from others in which remarkable turnaround is unexpected, because the Wounded Vets do not leave survivors...they kick managers to the curb. The only reasonably hopeful outcome for you is that you beat them, and survive. It is important to remember that some of these Vets might have actually performed well in the past and may have redeemable qualities.

What Will Team Dynamics Look Like?

Team dynamics of the Wounded Vets are something between a down and out group of homeless drunks and a pack of wolves. They have a secret handshake dating back to that convention in 1978 and the matching polo shirts the company handed out in 1988. They enable one another in their daily ineffectiveness, and fiercely defend one another against anyone who might be a threat. It would probably be better for you if they just sat there hunched over, passive, unkempt, and frumpy, but this group is capable of remarkable activity in the face of opposition. Some Wounded Veterans' teams are headed by a particularly loathsome leader who has been anointed evil dictator of this delusional group of revolutionaries. The rest of the team looks to him for guidance and assurance that they will be protected no matter how obstinate their behavior or dismal their daily results.

> It would probably be better for you if they just sat there hunched over, passive, unkempt, and frumpy, but this group is capable of remarkable activity in the face of opposition. Some Wounded Veterans' teams are headed by a particularly loathsome leader who has been anointed evil dictator of this delusional group of revolutionaries.

You will need to protect newcomers or non-Wounded Vets from ostracism. As you bring in the Replacements to round out the team, you need to ensure that they don't get chased out, or worse, taken in by the Wounded Veterans. Your culture must prevail, and in order for that to happen, you need to nurture it while you kill off the old culture. This begins by hiring professionals with a wholly different outlook on work than the Wounded Vets. Badass with experience will certainly run Retread out of the picture entirely, as he's willing to call him on every hyperbolic claim or bullshit story. As you begin to instill a modern mindset of success into these guys one employee at a time, the useless Vets on your team will either sink, swim, or preferably, get eaten by the sharks.

How Can You Maximize Your Time?

Your effectiveness will be measured by the speed with which you can hold these Vets accountable, expose them for the frauds they are, and send them out to pasture. So your time should be spent instituting strict behavioral standards, keeping impeccable records of the Veterans' failure or ability to meet those standards, and beating a path to HR's door with evidence you hope will lead to their dismissal if they fail. One chance you have to expedite matters and shock a Veterans' team into productivity by chopping off its head in the early days of your tenure—that is, swiftly removing the de facto leader of the team and scaring the other members straight. If de facto leadership is not immediately obvious (and it often is not), take some time early to interview others and learn where the power center is located. Whom do they respect most on the team? Whom would they recommend for team leadership? Is that person a viable option for positive change or will he just perpetuate the awful mindset that is currently the status quo?

Special Policy Considerations:

We all know the rules of engagement when dealing with bullies—stand up to them, hold your ground, and once you fatten a lip they'll go running home to mama. Dealing with Wounded Veterans is similar, except they're a bit more savvy than the schoolyard bully, and punching them in the mouth is frowned upon in most corporate environments.

- **DEEP LINES IN THE SAND:** We all know the rules of engagement when dealing with bullies—stand up to them, hold your ground, and once you fatten a lip they'll go running home to mama. Dealing with Wounded Veterans is similar, except they're a bit more savvy than the schoolyard bully, and punching them in the mouth is frowned upon in most corporate environments. Instead, you need to firmly and clearly state your expectations and the consequences for failing to meet them. Once they fail, you must be able to follow through on the stated consequences or these Vets will expose you as a powerless, punchless boss, and send you running home to *your* mama.

- **RECOGNIZE NEW BEHAVIOR:** Every once in a while, one of these Veterans might surprise you and engage in behavior that is fully in line with what you want to see. You have to seize on those moments and recognize the shit out of them. You never know... maybe they'll like your response and perform a bit more. Getting your Burnout to upgrade to Legend, or Slacker to recast himself as Player is a huge win, and can kickstart the transformation of your team. It becomes even easier if you are able to replace Asshole or Retread with a Badass or even a Future that you have the time to train and insulate from the poison of the other Vets.

Wounded Vets
Water Cooler Chatter

YOU: Hey team, thought I'd catch you guys here. Was wondering if we could get together this afternoon for a meeting?

RETREAD: Who changed the candy selection in the machine on the first floor? I like Chuckles and now they are gone.

BURNOUT: I love those things. Who took them out? Back in '88 I used to eat them every day. What grade were you in back in 1988, Boss? Third?

SLACKER: Hey, I am going to lunch after this. I could swing over to the Price Club and get them on my way back. The lines are usually long there so....

YOU: Um... team?

ASSHOLE: With those teeth of yours, Retread, you should cut out sweets entirely. And Burnout, your fat old ass should have quit eating candy once you lost that Jane Fonda workout video.

SLACKER: That reminds me, I have a dentist appointment tomorrow. It will probably take all day.

YOU: Okay, so maybe we'll shoot for tomorrow…thanks guys.

inventory management system.

Opened music CDs/DVDs/audio books may not be returned, and can be exchanged only for the same title and only if defective. NOOKs purchased from other retailers or sellers are returnable only to the retailer or seller from which they are purchased, pursuant to such retailer's or seller's return policy. Magazines, newspapers, eBooks, digital downloads, and used books are not returnable or exchangeable. Defective NOOKs may be exchanged at the store in accordance with the applicable warranty.

Returns or exchanges will not be permitted (i) after 14 days or without receipt or (ii) for product not carried by Barnes & Noble or Barnes & Noble.com.

Policy on receipt may appear in two sections.

Return Policy

<u>With a sales receipt or Barnes & Noble.com packing slip</u>, a full refund in the original form of payment will be issued from any Barnes & Noble Booksellers store for returns of undamaged NOOKs, new and unread books, and unopened and undamaged music CDs, DVDs, and audio books made within 14 days of purchase from a Barnes & Noble Booksellers store or Barnes & Noble.com with the below exceptions:

A store credit for the purchase price will be issued (i) for purchases made by check less than 7 days prior to the date of return, (ii) when a gift receipt is presented within 60 days of purchase, (iii) for textbooks, or (iv) for products purchased at Barnes & Noble College bookstores that are listed for sale in the Barnes & Noble Booksellers

Barnes & Noble Booksellers #2771
1400 Biddle Road
Medford, OR 97501
541-858-0203

STR:2771 REG:006 TRN:0209 CSHR:Marria M

Bare Knuckle People Management: Creating
  9781935618485   N
  (1 @ 14.95)   14.95
TOTAL   14.95
VISA DEBIT   14.95
  Card#: XXXXXXXXXXXXX2214

A MEMBER WOULD HAVE SAVED   1.50

Thanks for shopping at
Barnes & Noble

101.28A   09/09/2012 08:31PM

CUSTOMER COPY

Team #5

The Rookies

Who's on the Team?

The Rookies are a team composed mostly of, well, rookies. Rookies could be recent college grads new to the workforce, new industry players, or even experienced workers who are just new to the company. The point is that they're new. They don't know where the bathrooms are, or what appropriate attire is on casual Fridays, or how to answer questions about the company's core product line, or even what to do in the morning after they turn their computer on and check their e-mail. These guys are so green it's hard to differentiate them from a group of outsiders in for a tour of headquarters. We're talking newbies here—young, dumb, full of questions, inexperienced—who are prone to making boneheaded mistakes.

What's in It for You?

While managing the Rookies requires hours of arduous work, the rewards can be great. First, expectations for your team's performance will be tempered, so anything north of those expectations will put you in an excellent light. Second, and perhaps more importantly, the Rookies represent the block of clay that wannabe managers fantasize about molding into legendary corporate works of art. It is management in its purest form.

With Rookies, you can take all of your theoretical toys out for a spin, transfer knowledge to those who hunger for it, train them from the ground up, and shape a group of winners. If you don't like the opportunity the Rookies offer you, you probably aren't meant for management.

What Can You Reasonably Expect?

Realistically, the Rookies can deliver slow gains early on, and, assuming you can hang on to your developing upstarts, exponential growth later on. Your challenge will shift from getting them up and running to keeping them engaged, while inculcating into them the values you want them to have. Rookies will eat up your time, so be prepared to work long, grueling hours in which you'll find yourself engaged in minutiae you thought you left behind years ago. The silver lining? Maybe a refresher course in policies and procedures is just the thing to snap you out of some bad habits you've developed.

> *With Rookies, you can take all of your theoretical toys out for a spin, transfer knowledge to those who hunger for it, train them from the ground up, and shape a group of winners. If you don't like the opportunity the Rookies offer you, you probably aren't meant for management.*

What Will Team Dynamics Look Like?

Team dynamics for Rookie teams can run all over the map, because Rookies come in so many varieties. You will have a Noodler Jr. burying himself in the weeds. God willing, you will have a Franchise Jr. (or Future) picking up things and kicking ass right out of the shoot. You'll have Badass Jr. telling Noodler Jr. to take his weeds and shove them up his ass. And yes, you'll have Baby Inappropriate trying his best to keep the frat house alive.

Rest assured, no matter what personality they develop they will be vying for your attention, sizing each other up as they jockey for position, and clinging together helplessly in a corner of the cafeteria. You are mother hen to these little chicks, and they will be looking to you for direction and at each other for best friends and archrivals.

How Can You Maximize Your Time?

You need face time in front of your Rookies. Frequent standing team meetings and trainings will expedite their learning and ensure they're getting it in equal doses so you can begin gauging who's developing at what rates. You need to spend lots of time with your people on the job, so you can see them in action and give them real-time feedback on their performance. Remember, they have no idea what they're doing. So while most managers can attend interdepartmental meetings and prepare sexy market analyses to present to upper management, you need to show your Rookies how the hell to do their job. If you don't do it, they will learn it themselves and most likely screw it up beyond all recognition.

Special Policy Considerations:

- **MICROMANAGEMENT IS YOUR FRIEND:** In our opinion, the whole notion of micromanagement has gotten a bum rap, particularly when it comes to newbies. Look, if you have a Rookie team, by definition, they'll need extremely tight monitoring (read: micromanagement), otherwise they're entirely too likely to veer off course. You'll obviously need to consider what's appropriate for your particular team and your particular style, but you might consider the following, depending on the nature of your business:

- Twice daily (morning and evening) touch-base meetings or check-in calls (particularly if your team members work off-site);
- Daily or weekly minimum activity requirements (e.g., number of outbound calls made, clients serviced, projects completed, etc.);
- Monday morning and/or late Friday team meetings; and
- Weekly field/floor/call-observation periods to monitor professionalism.

If your Rookies find this monitoring oppressive, then list for them objective hurdles that, if overcome, would free them from your intense oversight. As long as your policy is clearly communicated and team members see a way out that's within your control, you likely won't receive much pushback. After all, as Rookies, they're desperate to know what it will take for them to be successful. And if someone isn't willing to play along out of the gates, chances are they aren't long for your world anyway. Plus, if you handle this correctly, they'll think you walk on water.

> *As Rookies, they're desperate to know what it will take for them to be successful. And if someone isn't willing to play along out of the gates, chances are they aren't long for your world anyway.*

- **BUILDING THE TEAM...BUILDING THE CUL-TURE:** The inexperienced nature of the Rookies calls for intentional actions from you to drive them together as a team and start to shape the culture you want. Plan periodic lunch or drink outings in which you pick up the tab. Get them talking informally about life outside of work and what their interests are. We know it sounds hokey and maybe even a pain in the ass, but cohesiveness will be your friend because it increases the likelihood that people will stay in their job, improves team communication and efficiency, and creates a sense of interdependence that reduces your need to meddle in day-to-day matters that affect individuals (i.e., they feel increasingly comfortable turning to each other). Finally, because you are shaping the culture, you can ensure it includes the components you find most critical to success, like attention to detail, seeing tasks through to the end, and customer service.

Rookie
Water Cooler Chatter

ROOKIE 1: Has anyone seen Boss?

ROOKIE 2: I saw him at lunch.

ROOKIE 3: You got to eat lunch with Boss? Are you serious? Oh, man.

ROOKIE 2: No, he was at a lunch with his fellow managers. I was just at a nearby table with other nobodies.

ROOKIE 3: He was? What were they talking about? Were they talking about us? What was Boss eating? Was it healthy? I bet it was healthy. He always has something healthy to eat. Oh, I just love him.

ROOKIE 1: Towel off, girl. He's just a man, and he puts his pants on one leg at a time in the morning, just like everyone else does.

ROOKIE 3: Oh, not Boss. No, sir. He puts his pants on two legs at a time in the morning. I swear it.

A WHISTLER-IN-TRAINING ROOKIE (popping out from behind a plant, recorder in hand): Rookie 3, how in the world would you know how Boss puts his pants on in the morning?

ROOKIE 3: Oh, Heavens, Whistler. I just...I mean...I know you look for...I was just making an innocent...oh, dear.

A MR. I-IN-TRAINING ROOKIE (exiting from a custodian's closet, where he was lurking, doing God knows what): So, you're sleeping with Boss. Unbelievable.

ROOKIE 1: Oh brother...can someone please just tell me where Boss is right now? I have a new client and he's asking me questions I have no clue how to answer.

PART IV
GETTING THE CALL

Your First 30 Days
as a Manager

Many of you reading this book are not yet managers, but you've been slated for management, and have been assured that your time will come when a position opens. And suddenly, one day, in the middle of a typical, run-of-the-mill work week, your phone will ring, and your boss's boss will be on the other end telling you "congratulations," that "you made it," and that "you start next week." Oh shit.

Once you get the call, so many practical and logistical concerns take over. You need to alert your customers or project partners. You need to transfer your stuff to a new office. You might even need to move to a new city. These are real, time-consuming, and in some cases, life-altering activities.

What most brand-new managers do is jump with two feet into their new role, figuring they'll do with their team sort of what their favorite managers did with them—learn as they go and get a little training at some point to smooth out the rough edges. There's nothing glaringly wrong with this approach (although you already know our take on packaged leadership training workshops), but by subscribing to it, you fail to consider one crucial element in the new manager's process—who the hell will you be managing and what's the best way to manage them? Failing to consider the team you're inheriting, and how to shape your policies accordingly, will cost you ramp-up time, productivity, and possibly head count.

The key for any new manager looking to make a smooth transition and deliver results right out of the gate is to START right:

What most brand-new managers do is jump with two feet into their new role, figuring they'll do with their team sort of what their favorite managers did with them— learn as they go and get a little training at some point to smooth out the rough edges.

- Survey the landscape
- Tailor the team policies and strategy to fit
- Announce the plan
- Roll out the plan
- Tweak the plan based on the first thirty days

Not sure what the hell we're talking about? Let's explain.

Imagine for a moment that you get the call to manage a team starting exactly one week from today. Here's our suggestion for giving yourself an effective START:

Survey the Landscape

Survey the Management

As soon as you hang up the phone—well, after you squeal for a few minutes and call your mom to let her know your college tuition wasn't a total loss after all—you need to start understanding what hand you've been dealt. Provided he wasn't ousted amid a controversy cloud, the team's outgoing manager is a great place to begin your survey. Ask him for his off-the-record take of the team as a whole as well as the dirt on each of the individual characters.

Some questions you'll want answers to:

- How has the team performed historically? Are there trends to watch for? Seasonal peaks or valleys? Contests and incentive programs that seem to particularly motivate them?

- Who are the team's Starting Five, Utility Players, Benchwarmers, and Trading Block candidates? Why does the outgoing manager classify each as such? Are there any worth shedding to make the team more effective?

- Who are the team's power brokers? How does their influence impact the group? What's the best way of dealing with them?

- What is each character's tenure?

- Are there obvious skills gaps that need to be filled?

- What is the outgoing manager's boss like? How does he like information? How accessible is he? Does he appreciate the big picture, or is he more focused on short-term results?

If you don't have access to the outbound manager, get whatever answers you can from your new boss, other executives, or a confidant who is familiar with that particular team.

You'll also want to gather some formal, objective data. Be sure to ask for quantitative reports, annual reviews, and the like. Look, neither the objective data nor the anecdotal manager reports alone will tell the whole story, but by collecting more information, you will start connecting the dots for yourself. You'll begin seeing trends jump off the page. As a fresh set of eyes on this team, you will see things differently than those who lived in the team on a day-to-day basis.

Finally, many managers get promoted to manage the team they were just a part of. While this has some obvious benefits—you know the players, you are familiar with the office executives, lateral departments, etc.—there are also obvious tensions.

Imagine, for example, if you successfully competed for the manager position against one or more players you'll soon be managing. Yikes! How will you deal with these inevitably awkward dynamics? What if they try to sabotage your efforts? Chances are they won't want you to succeed. Will you sit them down individually and have the heart-to-heart? Maybe you could enlist (read: bribe) them by telling them you will recommend them for a management post if they work with you and perform out of the gates.

> *There are no black-line rules on this stuff… give it some thought and come to a resolution that works for you and maximizes the likelihood of the team's (and your) success.*

You'll now be boss of your Thursday night drinking buddies—the ones you also used to join for Friday afternoon golf on the company's dime. You value their friendship, but now they report to you. Will you sit them down and come to terms with how to handle the inevitable "hard conversations" about performance and corner cutting? And can you carve out a plan to maintain your social relationship, or is it best to put it on ice during the first thirty days?

Look, there are no black-line rules on this stuff. These are incredibly hard and blurry issues that are very context- and individual-specific. We're not recommending that you make the call one way or another…we're just recommending that you give it some thought and come to a resolution that works for you and maximizes the likelihood of the team's (and your) success. That's all.

Survey the Team

You might ask to speak with one or more of the current team members. Find out their view of the team—how it performs, what seems to work and what doesn't, what they recommend as a management style, what they like/dislike about their outgoing manager. We know what you're thinking…why would we recommend that you speak with these peons? What could they possibly know about management?

We're not suggesting you take what they say as gospel, but consider this: what they say is another data point that will help you shape how you approach this new team. Look, even if what they say turns out to be complete bullshit, at least you learn that they either have terrible judgment or intentionally tried to mislead you—either of which is useful in your future dealings with them. Knowledge is power.

Tailor Policy and Strategy to Fit the Team

Once you know who you've got and what scene you're walking into, you can start shaping your team's policy. Determine:

- Will you have standing weekly team meetings?
- Will you demand regular and frequent check-ins with you?
- Will you have Franchise Forgiveness Factor rules in place or will you treat them all the same way?
- Will you carefully define roles or do you expect all your soldiers to be generalists so they can easily fill in for one another at a moment's notice?

You will want to be as clear and thorough as possible as you flesh out your overarching policies, because they're going to shape the major decisions that will be flying at you the minute your post begins.

Announce Policies and Strategy

You will probably want to present your strategy to your new boss. This will:

a) give him a heads-up about what you're planning to do and a chance to recommend tweaks;

b) help you appear thoughtful, diligent, and organized from the get-go; and

c) give you a run through to work out any kinks before delivering it to your most critical audience—your new team.

You should give some thought to how you roll this out to your team. Depending on some of the dynamics you unearth during the Survey stage, you might want to prepare some individual team members for what's coming in advance, or do a cheesy over-the-top kickoff to announce the arrival of a completely new guard. Imagine, for example, that you were hired to manage a loose collection of Slackers who were being carried by a Franchise and a Player. You are going to need to come in with the hammer on the Slackers, but you might want let Franchise and Player know your plan before the big kickoff meeting so you don't shock them into a new job search.

Roll Out the Plan

This is either going to be the easiest part or the hardest part. Close your eyes, press the button, and hope like hell it works. We're kidding—a bit. You don't have to close your eyes, but we do essentially encourage you to let the plan ride for thirty days or so. Rome wasn't built in a day, and neither will your team. Everyone will need to adjust to the new regime, work out the old and conform to the new, and generally find its new level.

Tweak the Plan if Necessary

On the one-month anniversary of your start date, you should have some useful data and be better equipped to optimize your plan further. Perhaps your plan has helped create a bump in productivity from a good handful of your reports that warrants a reduction in oversight from you.

START-STOP-CONTINUE

Want to be a bit brave? Ask your team members for their sense of how you're doing. Host a Start-Stop-Continue exercise, in which your team members sit together and list all the things they would like you to Start, those they would like you to Stop, and those they would like you to Continue doing. Now, this isn't for every manager or every team, but it can be a very nonthreatening way for your team to provide you with some useful information about how your team is measuring you.

Throughout this book, we have urged you to take stock of your people. In this section, we are trying to get your management career started on the right foot by having you take stock before you even step into the role. You need not incorporate the entire START program to find success, but increasing your awareness of the situation you've been hired into, and tailoring your plan accordingly, can only serve to improve the likelihood of a clean transition to management.

Management would be so easy if it were like all the "leadership gurus" say—wrap your team in big frequent group hugs, give them healthy doses of gold stars, and tell them they're all winners.

Gloves Off

Management would be so easy if it were like all the "leadership gurus" say—wrap your team in big frequent group hugs, give them healthy doses of gold stars, and tell them they're all winners. Just by picking up this book, you told us that you either never subscribed to the gurus in the first place, or you tried their recommendations and recognized their limitations.

Management is hard work. You have to find out what makes each of your people tick, and leverage that information to get as much as you can from each. You have to study the dynamics of your team and carefully craft a set of policies accordingly. And even if you do this, you might not get it right. People can be hard to read. Unforeseen variables can pop up out of nowhere and instantly render your plans useless. This is Ultimate Fighting—not pro wrestling—where the contact is real and the consequences for getting it wrong can be life altering.

This book doesn't make managing any easier, but helps you become more successful by teaching you to take the time to fully assess who you're managing, and treat your people accordingly. *Bare Knuckle People Management* is about helping you take off your management gloves and tear through the confining layers of tape and other bullshit that too often get in the way of managerial effectiveness.

So go ahead and take off those management gloves.

Good luck!

What type of character are YOU?

GO ONLINE AND FIND OUT!

Now that you've learned more about the characters on your team, why not find out what sort of manager you are? Go to *www.bareknucklepeoplemanagement.com/assessment* and take your free online assessment today. At this site you'll also find useful articles and tips on how to manage your team more effectively. Oh, and tell a friend. It's free.

About the Authors

 **SEAN O'NEIL** is principal owner and CEO of One to One Leadership, a sales and management training and recruitment company. He presents regularly on sales, management, leadership, workplace dynamics, career development, team-building, and communication issues at national and regional conferences. O'Neil has been published or been featured in *The New York Times*, *The Wall Street Journal*, *Selling Power*, *Executive Decision*, and *Incentive Magazine*, among others. His clients include the National Basketball Association, Major League Soccer, Oakland Raiders, Royal Bank of Scotland, News Corp., ADP, Shearman & Sterling LLP, Cornell Presbyterian Hospital, and First Data.

Sean is a graduate of Duke University's School of Law and Fuqua School of Business.

He lives in Pelham Manor, N.Y., with his wife, Erin, and their four children.

JOHN KULISEK is president of The Norben Group, a sales and marketing firm specializing in the production, import and distribution of fine permanent botanicals that operates in the United States, China, and Hong Kong. Some of the many places his quotes and managerial philosophies have appeared in and on include *The Wall Street Journal*, Microsoft.com, and ABC News.

He lives in Tenafly, N.J., with his wife, Pamela, and children Zachary and Ariana.

ABOUT ONE TO ONE LEADERSHIP

One to One Leadership is a nationally recognized sales and management training company that has been training managers and salespeople throughout the United States since 1983. One to One specializes in customizing no-nonsense, practical and entertaining training programs for corporate clients. One to One is also known for designing and delivering impactful off-site team-building sessions and entertaining speaking engagements.